A Manual for Church Growth Surveys

A Manual for Church Growth Surveys

Ebbie C. Smith

Preliminary Edition

533 Hermosa Street • South Pasadena, Calif. 91030

Copyright © 1976 by the William Carey Library

All rights reserved.

No part of this book may be used or reproduced in any manner whatsoever without written permission, except in the case of brief quotations embodied in critical articles and reviews.

In accord with some of the most recent thinking in the academic press, the William Carey Library is pleased to present this scholarly book which has been prepared from an author-edited and author-prepared camera-ready manuscript.

Library of Congress Cataloging in Publication Data

```
Smith, Ebbie C
    A manual for church growth surveys.

    Bibliography: p.
    1. Church growth--Handbooks, manuals, etc.
I. Title.
BV652.25.S55            254'.5            75-25999
ISBN 0-87808-145-3
```

Published by the William Carey Library
533 Hermosa Street
South Pasadena, Calif. 91030
Telephone 213-799-4559

PRINTED IN THE UNITED STATES OF AMERICA

Dedicated to the Memory of

Roger Wayne Smith

Our 15-year old son who died in an accident on an East Java highway, July 2, 1973, while this manual was in preparation

Contents

Foreword ix

Introduction xi

CHAPTER

1	Introducing Church Growth Surveys	1
2	Understanding Church Growth Surveys	5
3	Beginning a Church Growth Survey	16
4	Getting the Facts of Growth	26
5	Objectifying the Facts of Growth	55
6	Digesting the Facts of Growth	79
7	Making Decisions Based on the Survey	96
8	Implementing the Decisions	102
9	Conclusion	112

Appendix A Table 1. Average Annual Growth Rate Chart   117

Appendix A	Table 2. Check List for Church Growth Surveys	118
Appendix B	Helpful Materials for Church Growth Surveys	123
Appendix C	Distributing the Results of a Church Growth Survey	129

Foreword

The Church in the Western world is recovering from the spiritual depression of the last thirty years. Shock of loss of empire is wearing off. Neurotic preoccupation with Christian unity is giving place to an interest in unity that is more balanced and healthy. Christians are recognizing that transfer of authority to younger Churches goes forward best with increased missionary sendings to the huge unevangelized portions of the three billion who have yet to believe. Insistence that Christian obedience is exhausted in social action is being seen as a considerable exaggeration. The unswerving purpose of God for the salvaton of men's souls is being again recognized and hence Christians are resolving to serve the whole man-spirit as well as flesh. The truth that God has revealed one way of salvation--through faith in Jesus Christ according to the Bible--is resounding through the gatherings of the Redeemed. The growth and extension of the Church into every new generation and into every thousand of every segment of every society (urban and rural, Chinese, African, American, European and Indian, rich and poor, educated and illiterate) is being emphasized as our Lord intends that it should be.

At just this time, Dr. Ebbie C. Smith's *Manual for Church Growth Surveys* renders a notable service. It is by all odds the most comprehensive and sensible guide available. It tells how to launch a survey so that the organization doing it will regard it as its own and will implement its findings. It describes pitfalls and shows how to avoid them. It is usable by churches of varying polities. In short, this manual is a milestone in church growth thinking and practice.

Church growth surveys are a valuable part of the current spiritual rebound. Tens of thousands of them are being undertaken. Congregations, associations, presbyterians, conferences, synods, and missions are reviewing the church planting task which God has given them. Time, money, prayer, and sweat are being spent on these measurements of the height, depth, breadth, and durability of literally thousands of cases of church growth. All this treasure will be spent to better advantage if this manual is carefully read and its counsels are followed.

> Are you going to spend 20 hours (or 2000) on a church growth survey?
> First spend two hours on this book.
>
> Are you going to invest $20 (or $20,000) on digging out the facts?
> First invest in this book.
>
> Have you squeezed the maximum benefit out of your last survey?
> Read Smith and discover new ways to do so.
>
> Insure your investment.
> Study *A Manual for Church Growth Surveys*.

Be a better steward of the grace of God.

Donald McGavran
School of World Mission
Fuller Theological Seminary
Pasadena, California

Introduction

Someone said that "status quo" is a fancy title for the mess we're in. It is difficult to know whether we are indeed in a mess in missions (as many suggest) or in a march to sure victory (as most reports from missionaries insist) without the accurate facts that can be garnered by a careful survey.

A movement so vast, so important and so expensive surely deserves better than indiscriminate accusations from its detractors and—equally—better than good-willed but uninformed defense by its friends. The movement itself has much to gain from careful, accurate, relevant surveys of its personnel, its policies and its productivity. Such studies will surely help vindicate and substantiate the beneficent effects while enabling all those involved to improve the total performance and to "tune the magnificent machine" to peak performance on today's superhighways of opportunity.

Dr. Ebbie Smith writes on this subject from the richest fund of academic knowledge and field experience that I know of among Southern Baptist missionaries. He has spent fourteen years in Indonesia, a land of unusual opportunity and growth, especially during the last ten years (1965-1975). He poured hard work and careful thought into those years. As our mission sensed the importance of planned work (in contrast with uncritically doing what has always been done or simply reacting to the push and pull of each day as it arrives), Dr. Smith (Th.D., Southwestern Seminary, 1961) enrolled at the Institute of Church Growth at Fuller Seminary to garner all possible benefit from the insights of McGavran and company.

As part of that study program he wrote *God's Miracles: Indonesian Church Growth*. It was the foundation on which the mission further projected its self-study. He was chairman of the survey committee whose work led to significant, forward looking plans for great church growth. This was completed in 1971.

In 1972 he was invited to the Philippines to gather together the results of several years of survey and self-study by the Southern Baptist mission there. He gave very helpful counsel to the missionaries there as they restructured their work for greater productivity.

We've long needed this book. Read it, heed it, put it to work for the glory of God.

R. Cal Guy
Professor of Missions
Southwestern Baptist Theological Seminary
Ft. Worth, Texas

1
Introducing Church Growth Surveys

Is your Church's* membership growing, stagnating, or declining? Is it growing (or declining) at the same rate in all regions? What methods are producing growth?

How does your group's growth compare with others? Are some segments of the population responding more readily to the Gospel? Is your group serving the more responsive peoples?

Are the resources of your Church being employed in such a way as to attain maximum growth? Do you know the rate of growth for your group over the last ten years? What could stimulate your Church to more adequate growth?

---
*The term "Church" is variously used. Written with a capital "C" the term means either the Church Universal or more often, a denomination or convention-- such as the methodist Church in Nigeria. Written with a small "c" it usually means a local congregation or is used as an adjective. However, what is said here about a Church is usually equally true for a church, a missionary society, or any other religious group undertaking a Church Growth Survey.

Answers to such questions contain imperative information for every religious group. Unfortunately, seldom is such information accurately known or diligently sought. The growth of churches will be enhanced when, and only when, accurate information about church growth is assimilated and put to use. Church Growth Surveys are one of the most effective ways of obtaining this information.

Every religious organization must look closely and objectively at its progress (or lack of progress) and at its methods. Growth should be compared with that of other groups working in the same areas. The facts of growth, stagnation, or decline must be seriously sought and honestly faced. Church Growth Surveys help in the discovery and appreciation of these imperative facts.

Finding, facing, and evaluating the facts of growth is a spiritual undertaking. There are few more wasteful procedures than continuing year after year with no genuine effort to analyze methods, evaluate results, or seek more productive ways. It is therefore imperative for every religious organization to analyze what it is doing, how it is doing it, and ways the harvest can be increased. In fact, refusal to seek and act on the facts of growth may be unfaithfulness to God.

Church Growth Surveys, described in this manual, discover the facts of growth, help in their interpretation, and thereby constitute a foundation for needed change. Surveys, having a definite purpose, are eminently practical. They aim not to merely supply academic information, but to provide a basis for more effectively attaining God's will for world evangelization.

There are various types of Church Growth Surveys. One type involves a single person (or a small group) studying a single church or denomination in a certain area. Roy Shearer's, *Wildfire: Church Growth in Korea*, and Paul Enyart's, *Friends in Central America*, are examples of this type of survey. Comparative data is important in such studies but primarily they relate to one specific Church tradition.

Another type of survey considers all, or most of, the Churches in a limited area. This type is much more comparative in nature. It may be conducted by an individual or by a small group. Examples are:

Gilbert Olson's, *Church Growth in Sierra Leone*, William Read's, *New Patterns of Church Growth in Brazil*, and A. L. Tuggy and R. Toliver, *Seeing the Church in the Philippines*.

Then, some surveys consider church growth over a very wide region. Perhaps the most notable of these surveys is by William Read, V. M. Monterroso and H. A. Johnson, *Latin American Church Growth*. Such extensive surveys usually require the work of several collaborators and significant funding. The study resulting in *Latin American Church Growth* was commissioned by The School of World Mission and Institute of Church Growth, Fuller Theological Seminary, and was supported by the Lilly Endowment, Inc. Hopefully, studies of this nature will be possible for other major regions of the world.

Perhaps the most effective type of survey involves an entire group in self-study. Such a survey is a joint effort in every sense of the word. The joint venture type of survey gathers the same types of material and uses the same techniques as the other surveys. It differs in the self-study feature, the use of outside evaluators, and the definite goal of decision-making. This type of survey includes specific plans for implementing decisions and results. Self-studies promise increased effectiveness in augmenting church growth.

This manual presents methods and techniques that can be used in any type of survey. It relates primarily, however, to studies of denominations, missions, or other groups who conduct self-studies. Still, the suggestions can be easily modified and adapted for use in every type of survey and by any type of group--a local church, a society, or an entire denomination. Because the suggestions can be adapted to various types of groups, the manual employs the term "group under study," to signify the Church, mission, local congregation, or other entity that conducts the survey.

The methods of adaptation vary with the purpose of the survey and the group studied. A Church conducting a survey will select the committee and carry out the survey in the usual patterns of work for that denomination. Many have done this. Most recently the Evangelical Covenant Church in America has raised $5 million dollars in a special "Giving for Growth" program. In such a case the decision meeting would likely consist of a congress, convention, or a special meeting of representatives of the congregations. On the other hand, a mission would likely use a mission meeting, attended by most of its members, to draw conclusions and make decisions based on the survey. A church would likely use a business session or some other church meeting for the evaluation and decision making phases of the survey.

Note that the title of this study is "A Manual for Church Growth Surveys," and not "The Manual." This manual is not exhaustive. Other techniques can and will be employed. It is hoped that these plans and guides will be used by Churches, missions, and local congregations to find the facts of growth and that these facts, rightly interpreted, will stimulate Church Growth.

The next chapter sets forth an all-important first step--understanding Church Growth Surveys.

2
Understanding Church Growth Surveys

Effective surveys begin with understanding Church Growth Surveys. This understanding includes the nature of surveys, their values, and the psychology that often attends them.

WHAT CHURCH GROWTH SURVEYS ARE

Church Growth Surveys are studies of the methods and results of Church activity together with definite recommendations for increasing results. Surveys consist of techniques for objectively finding and interpreting the facts of growth. They use these techniques to find and explain the advances, plateaus, and declines in the group's growth. The survey strives to provide a foundation for change leading to more effective evangelism.

Surveys are objective. Effective surveys discover the way things really are. Promotional thinking and defensive attitudes are laid aside. No one opinion, conviction, or theory is championed. The study strives to set forth how the churches have grown, when and for what reasons periods of advance or stagnation have occurred, and how the growth of the group compares with other organizations.

Loss of objectivity prevents a survey from its greatest effectiveness. Only accurate information provides the proper foundation for effective advance. Therefore, Surveys must be objective.

Surveys are specific. Effective surveys concentrate on a definite group or groups. Other organizations working in the same area and among the same peoples are considered for comparative purposes but the survey concentrates on finding the facts and providing recommendations for the group under study. Thus, defining the entity to be studied is an important beginning point for a survey.

Surveys center on church growth. Effective surveys find and interpret the facts of growth in order to answer the dual questions: "Why has the Church grown or failed to grow?" and, "How can growth be stimulated and increased?" Church growth should not be, however, defined too narrowly. Church growth relates to far more than the simple numerical increase of membership.

Church growth theory considers effective evangelism. It emphasizes discipling the peoples of the world and recognizes that the most effective evangelism is realized through planting congregations into which the Christians can be incorporated and guided to spiritual maturity. Moreover, church growth theory insists that these Christians and congregations participate in the continuing opportunities for evangelism and service.

Clearly, all that the Church does influences church growth. The survey then, while centering on church growth, investigates every area of work from the vantage point of its relation to the increase of Christians and congregations and the spiritual maturing of both. Of central importance are questions such as, "How does medical, literature, social, or educational work relate to and influence church growth?" The survey of necessity studies everything the group is doing. It centers on the relation of Church activity to the growth (or lack of growth) of church membership and the increase (or decrease) of congregations.

To adequately study church growth, the survey must scrutinize every facet of work. Membership totals for both the entire Church and individual congregations for each year, along with figures on increase by baptism and by transfer, are carefully gathered. Rates of growth are calculated. The nature of growth is considered. Times of more and of less rapid advance are considered from the standpoint of "Why?"

The use of personnel, funds, and opportunities through the years is considered. Methods and their results are scrutinized. Effectiveness of differing approaches are compared. The survey investigates every phase of the work according to its relation to church growth.

Surveys are practical. Surveys have a purpose. Finding and interpreting the facts of growth are neither light nor unimportant tasks. They are, however, only preliminary. The purpose of gathering and interpreting facts is that of revealing areas in which the work can be strengthened and growth increased. Practically, surveys exist to advocate methods and changes that will result in more effective evangelization.

Ultimately, the survey seeks to bring the group to a realization of the actual situation, provide suggestions for needed changes, and lead in definite plans for implementing these plans. A survey reaches its objective only to the degree that it *results in needed changes, more effective evangelism, and more adequate church growth.*

THE VALUES OF CHURCH GROWTH SURVEYS

Only when convinced of its value will a group undertake a task of the magnitude of a Church Growth Survey. Experience has demonstrated that significant values are realized through surveys.

Surveys provide accurate information concerning growth or lack of growth. As stated previously, only accurate information can provide a foundation for effective advance. Surveys, correctly engaged, provide accurate information.

One group felt they were attaining good growth because of the steady advance of membership totals. However, a survey indicated that 41% of the membership growth came through transfers from other denominations. The accurate information resulted in the group's change of emphasis to reach out to the unchurched in a more effective manner. By providing accurate assessment of the situation, the survey played a significant part in formulating new plans.

Surveys provide actual data to test suggested reasons for growth or non-growth. Of the many reasons given for growth or non-growth, some are valid, but many are not. Only by carefully, objectively, and scientifically gathering and interpreting the facts can the valid reasons be separated from the invalid.

Dr. Donald McGavran reports a survey which corrected an inaccurate assessment of the reasons for growth of the Disciples of Christ Church in China. McGavran sought reasons for a spurt of growth this Church experienced in 1942. One missionary attributed the increased growth to the changing attitudes toward America and the introduction of agricultural teaching in the training school. A second missionary pointed out that several independent Churches became affiliated with the Disciples of Christ Church at that time (1970:124-25). The survey uncovered the true explanation of the growth spurt.

Surveys provide a corrective for inaccurate information. One writer intimated that the growth of the Baptist churches in Java was primarily the result of attracting members from other Churches and the use of missionaries as pastors for local congregations (Cooley 1968:45-48). A survey indicated that only 17% of the members of Baptist churches had ever been members of any other Church. Moreover, of fifty-four churches only three were led by missionary pastors in 1965 (Smith 1970:145-53). Thus, a more accurate assessment of the growth corrected an erroneous assumption.

Surveys provide vital information concerning the peoples served. Church growth takes place among people. Therefore, a thorough historical, anthropological, and sociological understanding of the people served is indispensible in projecting plans for increased church growth. Providing this background material is one of the major values of Church Growth Surveys. Max Randall's *Profile for Victory: New Proposals for Missions in Zambia*, is an especially significant example of the value of background material for missionary strategy.

Surveys provide an evaluation of the methods employed. Every method used by the group should be investigated. There should be no sense of criticism or fault finding involved. However, *when it is evident that some method has not resulted in significant church growth, or that an adjustment in method would likely increase effectiveness, faithfulness to the Lord of the Harvest demands that recommendations to that end be forthcoming.*

A willingness to evaluate honestly, analyze correctly, and adjust courageously is a prerequisite for

progress. A survey provides opportunity to study
the past in order to influence the future. As
methods and their results are scrutinized, the
strengths and weaknesses become apparent and new
methods are discovered.

   Joseph Wold's *God's Impatience in Liberia* is an
example of how the evaluation of methods can provide
a useful foundation for change. Wold's evaluation
indicates that meager growth resulted from the early
reliance on education as the main avenue for Lutheran
work in Liberia. He further describes the increasing
results as methods were adjusted (1968:97-110).
Another survey indicated that, at a critical time for
evangelism, the Bapists in Indonesia had assigned
61.9% of their evangelistic force to the two least
responsive areas in which they worked. This fact
led to the decision of deploying evangelists in the
more responsive areas. Thus, the evaluation of methods constitutes a major value of Church Growth Surveys.

   *Surveys provide a data-bank of church growth prin-
ciples and information*. Every church growth study
should be written so that it can become a part of the
rapidly increasing data-bank of church growth knowledge. Charles Bennett's *Tinder in Tabasco* clearly
reveals this value. Bennett's study indicates the
danger of overemphasizing the highly trained, ordained
ministry to the exclusion of the ministry of the entire body of Christ. Moreover, Bennett contributes
the principle of the importance of the laity in evangelism and church growth (1968:119).

   Dr. A. R. Tippett clearly states the principle of
continued outreach and the danger of overemphasizing
consolidation in his study, *Solomon Islands Christianity*. Tippett shows how the drive for "quality" can so
often lead to introversion and thereby inhibit growth.
Surveys are important to providing this bank of church
growth information.

Understanding Church Growth Surveys

Surveys provide a foundation of church growth understanding among the members of the group under study. The group, of necessity, considers a vast amount of church growth information during the course of the survey. This information constitutes a store of understanding of the principles that lead to church growth. This understanding influences future work. Comprehension of church growth principles and the ability to see the work from the church growth angle is spoken of as "Church Growth Eyes." Development of "Church Growth Eyes" is a significant contribution of Church Growth Surveys.

Surveys provide a springboard for needed change and new strategy. New effectiveness in evangelism is the chief purpose of surveys. Likewise, provision of a foundation or springboard for needed change and new strategy is the prime value of surveys. The facts of growth will point irresistibly toward needed changes. Investigating ways to effect these changes will lead to new strategy.

Roy Shearer's survey of the Presbyterian Church in Korea revealed clearly that the major growth had been experienced in the three northern provinces. This fact could have led to the strategy of increasing the evangelistic effort in those responsive areas (*Wildfire 1966:81-84*). B. V. Subbamma makes definite recommendations for evangelism among Hindus in Andhra Pradesh, India. She suggests creating new and separate congregations for each of the different social and ethnic groups rather than trying to evangelize everyone through only one type of congregation (1970: 52ff). Such recommendations should lead to new patterns of church growth and development.

One group, as a result of a survey, decided to move away from an over-reliance on subsidy and to attempt to establish a more self-perpetuating pattern. Another group moved to redeploy its evangelistic staff so as to reach more responsive mountain peoples.

Still another survey led to a new program of leadership training that provided training for leaders in an expanded evangelistic program. Such changes in plans and strategy constitute one of the most significant values of Church Growth Surveys.

Surveys provide new goals. Surveys often result in a willingness to try new ways. The vision of better paths and fuller harvest is often opened to the group. This new vision, embodied in definite goals and timetables, gives a freshness and direction to the work and lends greater efficiency.

The background study for one survey recommended a goal of 70,000 new Christians in ten years (Smith 1970:194). As a result of the full survey, the group adopted a goal of one million in ten years. This group, the Indonesian Baptist Mission, adopted this goal with the full conviction that it was not beyond the reach of the Lord of the Harvest. New goals, adopted as a result of surveys, constitute another important value of such studies.

Surveys provide a healthful climate for the work of the Holy Spirit. Considering past victories and defeats and looking toward future possibilities creates an atmosphere for repentance. As the group strides together for new light and better ways, the Holy Spirit has unique opportunities to create a new unity and bring about spiritual renewal. A new emphasis on spiritual life and spiritual ministry often emerges. As a result of surveys in several countries, a new emphasis on spiritual life, particularly among missionaries, has been apparent, according to W. R. Wakefield, Southeast Asia Area Representative for Southern Baptist Missions.

Surveys provide for more enlightened sharing with the home base. Too often, sharing results of missionary work with the supporting base takes the form of promotional thinking. Surveys provide new and more accurate information about the past and an enlarged vision for the future. The new plans, methods, and goals provide a valuable new dimension to missionary sharing with home supporters.

Surveys are valuable and vital techniques for all groups engaged in Christian service. Their primary values reside in their function of enhancing church growth. The values of surveys should stimulate every group to consider undertaking a Church Growth Survey.

THE PSYCHOLOGY OF SURVEYS

There is a psychology of surveys that sometimes inhibits, but more often enhances, their usefulness. Surveys are new. Consequently, to some they are attractive; to others they constitute a threat. There often develops around the idea of a Church Growth Survey a basic psychology--both positive and negative.

Negative elements in the psychology of surveys at times result in resistance to their use. These negative reactions are as honest and understandable as are positive feelings. Negative feelings should not be criticized. Rather, effort should be made to consider, respect, and minister to those who hold them.

Negative feelings toward a survey often spring from doubts, either of the value of such an undertaking in general, or of some of the facts or potential recommendations in particular. Others find themselves in disagreement with some of the survey's decisions. Such doubts create a more than ample basis for negativism.

Negative feelings are sometimes based on the results of previous surveys. Surveys, like all other methods, have their successes and their failures. Both valid decisions and mistakes are made. Reports from one survey often arouse negative feelings in other areas.

Further negativism revolves around the trauma of confronting past mistakes and failures. It is not easy to surrender one's work to the clear light of analysis. Some persons retreat from the clear implication of the facts into a negativism toward the entire idea of the survey.

Protectiveness and a desire to cling to previous patterns which have been partially successful often engender a spirit of negativism. This spirit is sometimes intensified by a fear of the new and possibly unproved methods sometimes recommended. This type of negativism is often experienced both by individuals on the field and by administrators at the home base.

Further negativism surrounds the final phase of implementing the decisions of the survey. It is easier to plan than to produce. As survey decisions come into the arena of action, difficulties and delays are often faced, giving rise to frustrations and doubts. Even though decisions have been reached together, there is sometimes evidence of changing feelings and "grumbling in the wilderness." Thus, frustrations during the period of implementing the decisions of the survey may add their weight of negativism.

Positive elements in the psychology of surveys make such efforts eminently worthwhile. A sense of achievement is among the more central positive elements of Church Growth Surveys. Individually and collectively the group gains the assurance that they faced up to the facts and made genuine efforts to find better ways. The new plans and goals lend a definite sense of accomplishment and potential release from past failures and pessimism.

Repentance constitutes a second major psychological and spiritual element in surveys. One group began their final survey report with a statement of repentance for mistakes in the previous pattern of work. Genuine repentance produces lasting change and is therefore a healthy factor. To see past errors should lead, not to despair or bitterness, but to new directions. These new directions constitute repentance.

The determination to follow the new plans and to reach the new goals is a further positive element in the psychology of surveys. The determination to follow those methods that will increase church growth is closely connected with this principle. Correctiveness, while never an easy step, produces increased harvest.

Many groups find a new cohesiveness as a result of surveys. As they work together and receive the experiences of a survey, the group often coalesces into a new unity. This new unity and cohesiveness is one of the most significant positive elements in the psychology of surveys.

CONCLUSION

Surveys are hard work. They are expensive. Both man hours and feelings are involved. A certain amount of conflict and negativism is often experienced. Still, surveys can be greatly used to help a group see its task more clearly, dedicate itself to that task more intensely, and seek ways of accomplishing that task more realistically.

Every suggestion in this manual will not apply to every survey or every group. One suggestion, however, has universal application: "Every religious group should undertake a Church Growth Survey." Ways of conducting such surveys are described in the following pages.

3
Beginning A Church Growth Survey

Church Growth Surveys, once begun, gather and interpret the facts of growth. Before reaching this point, however, the study must conclude several vital preliminaries. This chapter considers ways to get a survey started.

DETERMINING TO BEGIN A SURVEY

Surveys do not just happen. They begin when some group reaches the determination to find and act on the facts of growth and communicates this determination to their co-workers. These initiators must be persistent enough to get the survey started and yet careful not to engender or intensify resistance.

Surveys demand dedication and determination. It is easier to ignore problems and delay change. Only as there arises a dedication and willingness to seek the facts of growth and follow their revelations will a study be made.

SECURING SUPPORT FOR THE SURVEY

Since surveys reach their highest efficiency as joint projects, widespread support is a vital element. Should the survey be looked on as the idea and effort

Beginning A Church Growth Survey 17

of a small portion of the group only, the entire study will suffer. Wider participation and closer support predicts greater success.

At the same time the survey should include all segments of the population being studied in order to reach maximum effectiveness. Thus, when a Church initiates a survey, it should consider organizations that have close ties with it, such as a mission. When a Mission sponsors a survey, it should include the national Christians and Church. When denominational or mission leaders plan a survey, they should seek support from all the survey will affect. An individual conducting a study of a Church, a group of Churches, or churches, should gain permission, secure support, and establish a working relationship with the group to be studied.

Support is vital to a survey. However, complete support for any program is seldom reached. Waiting for total agreement and support before undertaking a survey would likely insure that no study would be made. Support is important; widespread support is helpful. Still, opposition, lack of interest, or even resistance should never be allowed to obstruct the promotion of a needed survey.

SELECTING THE STEERING COMMITTEE

Once a group determines to project a survey, it must provide leadership. A working committee best serves this purpose.

The committee must be composed of members who possess the abilities, characteristics, and training needed for survey work. No talent is more necessary than the ability to think clearly on evangelistic strategy. Committee members must be able to both plan and produce. They must be able to lead and stimulate. A background of achievement indicates that the members have some of the needed abilities.

Among characteristics needed by committee members, none is more important than the willingness to work. Surveys involve effort. Only those willing and able to give time and energy will contribute significantly.

A high degree of creativity and objectivity are other necessary characteristics. Willingness to hear and consider other opinions enhances the process of obtaining facts. Refusal to consider alternatives weakens the survey's influence. Furthermore, objectivity allows for more accurate assessment and interpretation of the facts of growth.

Courage is an indispensible trait for members of the steering committee. They must be willing to take a stand, even an unpopular one. They must be able to absorb criticism. They must be willing to suggest changes in the face of resistance and scorn.

There are needs of the committee that can be filled only by those with special training. Some members of the committee should have a good grasp of church growth principles. Knowledge of social research methods is valuable if some member of the group is trained in these techniques. Church growth principles and social research methods are of such value to a survey, that a period of study for some committee members in these areas is a good investment. Since the survey involves a great deal of communication, and eventually written reports, gifted and trained writers are an asset to the steering committee.

No one person will possess all of the abilities, characteristics, and training needed. Committee members should be selected to include as many of these gifts as possible. After selection, the committee assumes the overall leadership of the study.

The committee must be representative. Representativeness both allows the committee to better fulfill its duties and also enhances the acceptance of the survey findings.

The committee should be representative geographically. Much survey work is done on an area basis. Area representatives gather information from and communicate to their regions.

The committee should represent as many as possible of the types of work in which the group engages. Differing views on strategy, life styles, and other factors can be helpful on the steering committee. Care must be taken that the committee not become so large nor so divided as to become unwieldy or stymied by discord. The committee needs the advantage of wide representation.

The committee should have a chairman. He occupies a position of great significance. He must assume overall direction of every phase of the study. The chairman should be chosen well in advance of the survey year in order to prepare for the study. Two years in advance is not too early to select him.

The chairman must understand the principles of why churches grow or fail to grow. He must be dedicated to the cause of world evangelism and church development. He must have the respect of the group and be able to get things done. The chairman should' be prepared to dedicate at least one year, and perhaps more, to the conclusion of the survey.

It is no simple task to find one who combines leadership, dedication, training, knowledge, and opportunity to serve in this capacity. However, such men are available. Every group will likely discover several who can fill this important post.

The committee should be selected with care. It is advisable that the committee be selected at least one year before the final phase of the study. This early selection of both chairman and committee allows more adequate preparation, and more efficient implementation.

Selection of the steering committee should follow the procedures of the group under study. It should never, however, be simply a popularity contest. The selection of the steering committee can make or break the survey.

The committee provides direction and leadership for the survey. Gathering and sharing information, together with planning and carrying out plans will consume the time and energy of the committee. Only with aggressive and dedicated leadership can the survey reach its objectives.

PROVIDING BACKGROUND MATERIAL

Providing historical, sociological, and cultural materials constitutes one of the survey's first tasks. This material forms a foundation for the entire study as it relates how these historical, social, and cultural factors have affected and will affect the growth of the group under study. One year in advance of the final survey effort is not too early to distribute the background material which usually takes the form of a library research project.

The background study must center on and be relevant to church growth. Reliable information on the historical, social, anthropological, and religious situation relating to the group is imperative to any understanding of church growth. Valid plans for the future can only be formulated on the basis of accurate information on the past and sound data concerning the culture.

Background material focuses squarely on those factors affecting the planting and developing of growing churches. It should never be simply a historical or ethnological study. McGavran concludes:

...The student of church growth is highly selective. He gathers only those facts which are needed to understand the thrusts of growth and recession. Instead of presenting a profusion of data, most of it irrelevant as concerns the increase of Christians, he presents only data having something to do with his theme (1970:98).

The background material should contain historical, sociological, anthropological, and religious facts that relate to church growth. Church growth, while much more than a social or anthropological phenomenon, takes place within the differing societies of mankind. Therefore, to understand why churches grow (or fail to grow) it is imperative to understand the historical situation, the social structure, and the cultural milieu of the peoples among whom the Church is laboring (McGavran 1970:183).

Background material includes a history of the region in which the group is working. This is not simply a history but a church growth history. It isolates those historical factors affecting the growth of churches. Bennett's *Tinder in Tabasco* relates how the persecution of Christians in Tabasco between 1924 and 1935 resulted in increased church growth (1968:70ff). Political events surrounding the communist failure in Indonesia in 1965 stimulated growth in the churches of East Java (Cooley, 1968:90).

Also needed is a detailed history of the group under study. The various regions opened, the institutions established, and the general pattern of growth should be carefully noted. While this historical section will not attempt any detailed interpretation of the facts, it should present the group's history as a basis for later interpretation.

The social structure of the peoples served must be clarified and related to church growth. Social structure relates to the power structure, marriage customs, kinship lines, land rights, and many other cultural factors that influence church growth. The people of Madura in Indonesia have remained solidly Islamic and furiously resistant to Christianity due largely to the strong extended family units that make up Madurese social structure. These strong extended family units exert extreme pressure on members to remain in the accepted religious patterns, i.e. Islam. Christianity grows slowly in regions where to become a believer separates one from his people (Smith 1970: 33).

Background material relates the historical, religious and cultural factors to church growth. Finding ways to allow men to consider the Gospel is one of the purposes of background material. "The great obstacles to conversion are social, not theological. Great turning of Moslems and Hindus can be expected as soon as ways are found for them to become Christian without renouncing their brethren, which seems to them a betrayal" (McGavran 1970:191). To find and suggest ways to allow men a freedom to choose is the purpose of the background study in a survey.

The background material can be obtained in several ways. The group can use historical and anthropological materials already prepared. The growing bank of church growth studies opens this possibility in more and more areas. However, rarely does the background material of one survey exactly fit the needs of another.

Even if an existing study can be used, it usually requires adaptation, updating, and supplementing in order to meet the needs of the new survey. The important step of providing background material should not be slighted by merely accepting indiscriminantly an existing study.

The better method of securing the background study is commissioning some person or group to prepare it. Since such preparation involves extensive research and consequently a great amount of time, those commissioned should be provided with time and funds to conclude an in-depth study.

Patterns for preparing this background material are available in the many area studies of church growth that have been produced in recent years. These studies demonstrate how to select historical, social, religious, and political materials to cast light on church growth. All related to the survey should become familiar with several of these case studies.

The historical and anthropological material can be drawn from books and articles of general historical and ethnological interest. From traditional histories one draws the facts that relate to church growth. The anthropological and cultural facts are drawn from the ethnological literature that has been produced on most of the peoples of the world.

Before compiling historical and anthropological materials, the compilers should read carefully Chapter Ten of McGavran's *Understanding Church Growth* and Part III, or pages 117-147, of Tippett's *Verdict Theology in Missionary Theory* (Wm. Carey Library Edition). Both sources provide guidance in studying social structure and social change as it relates to church growth. Another indispensible source is Tippett's *Bibliography for Cross-Cultural Workers*. This bibliography lists various materials that can be used in a church growth survey.

The background materials should be distributed. As already indicated, the background material should be reproduced and made available to every member of the group as early as possible. Others will also be interested in this information. The material should be distributed and members of the group encouraged to carefully read and react to it. (See Appendix C).

ESTABLISHING A CHURCH GROWTH BASE

Effective communication of church growth principles is essential to the successful conclusion of a survey. Therefore, establishing an adequate understanding of church growth among the members of the group is an important step. The group, like the committee, must develop "church growth eyes."

A church growth base can be established by circulating books, articles, and reviews on church growth. A circulating library of church growth books can make this material available to members of the group without too great an outlay of money. Appendix B gives a list of helpful materials.

Some find it difficult to complete an entire book. Hence, an effective method of sharing church growth reading is the systematic distribution of articles and reviews. Each member of the group (or as many as possible) should be provided a special container in which to keep these church growth materials. Monthly, or bi-monthly articles and reviews should be distributed.

Sending materials at intervals has the advantage of emphasizing both the articles and the survey itself. To be presented a mass of material at one time is overpowering. Articles arriving at intervals are more likely to be read. They remind the members of church growth and the survey even when not thoroughly digested.

A church growth base can be established by holding church growth seminars. These seminars should be made available to as many members of the group as possible. Leaders well-versed in church growth principles should be secured to lead these seminars.

The seminars should be more than simple teaching sessions. There should be opportunities for questions, discussions, and sharing. Spiritual factors should be central in the seminar programs.

A church growth base can be established by translating church growth materials into national languages. The expanding body of church growth data must be made available to readers of every language. Providing these vital materials in the national languages is a significant service of a Church Growth Survey.

A church growth base can be established by setting up a clearing house for church growth materials. An office or person with responsibility for keeping the group aware of and informed about church growth thinking contributes greatly to the church growth base. Many will remain unaware of new ideas and writings unless their attention is directed to these materials. The clearing house can also provide for continuing research and study.

EMPHASIZING SPIRITUAL FACTORS

Church growth is a spiritual reality. While the theory of church growth makes full use of anthropological and sociological insight and techniques, it is basically a spiritual movement. The power for all church growth comes from the Holy Spirit. Therefore, the survey will at every point emphasize spiritual factors and anticipate spiritual harvest.

CONCLUSION

The survey is well-started when the group has reached a determination to make the study, has selected the steering committee, has begun the work of establishing a church growth base, has provided the needed background materials, and has determined to keep the spiritual central. Having reached this point, the stage is set for the fact-gathering phase of the survey.

4

Getting the Facts of Growth

Gathering the facts of growth is among the most demanding phases of the survey. Sociological research techniques, such as sampling, questionnaires, interviews, and coding, contribute significantly to this effort. Some surveys have profitably used computers.

Many of the facts of growth are numerical. An objective, numerical approach is indispensable for understanding church growth. To those who scorn the statistical approach, McGavran answers:

> To be sure, no one was ever saved by statistics; but then, no one was ever cured by the thermometer to which the physician pays such close attention. X-ray pictures never knit a single broken bone, yet they are of considerable value to phyicians in telling them how to put the two ends of a fractured bone together. Similarly, the facts of growth will not in themselves lead anyone to Christ. But they can be of marked value to any Church which desires to know where, when, and how to carry on its work so that maximum increase of soundly Christian churches will result (1970:84).

ISOLATING THE FACTS NEEDED

Church Growth Surveys demand a multitude of facts. Before setting forth techniques for gathering these facts, it is necessary to isolate the needed facts. A fuller discussion of these facts is found in Chapter Five of McGavran, *Understanding Church Growth* (1970).

The first body of facts relates to membership total figures. Virgil Gerber emphasizes the importance of membership statistics, calling them "the bedrock of data" necessary for diagnosing the health of a church (1973:43). Membership figures are needed for at least ten years--even longer for older Churches. Membership totals for: (1) the entire Church; (2) each geographical, cultural or administrative area; (3) each local congregation; (4) each homogeneous unit, are indispensable for understanding church growth.

Ideally, membership totals should include figures for each year. This is often impossible. Therefore, statistics are gathered for as many years as possible. Figures at times seem to reveal discrepancies. In time, however, the statistics will rectify themselves. Any year, or number of years, may be inaccurate. The general trend is, however, firm as a rock. Later entries correct earlier mistakes.

Membership figures must be refined for the sake of clarity and accuracy. One Church discovered the need for refining membership figures when it found its total remaining at about 9,500 for two consecutive years, although the congregations reported over 1,200 baptisms. The discrepancy was explained upon discovering that four large congregations had not reported the second year. A closer approximation of membership was gained by adding the previous year's total membership for these four congregations to the second year's figure. Careful refining of the facts lends accuracy and clarity.

Clarity and accuracy are also enhanced by careful attention to the meaning of membership. This is extremely important in comparative studies. Membership figures for some Churches consider only those who have made personal decisions to follow Christ; other Churches include as members those baptized as infants. For accuracy in comparative studies, it is well to use the term "membership" for those who have made definite commitments and use the term "community" for the total group, including those baptized as infants.

Clear and accurate membership statistics reveal periods of advance, stagnation, and decline. Reasons must be sought for these advances, plateaus and declines. Membership figures form the backbone of the Church Growth Survey.

Attention is called to the need for membership totals for each homogeneous unit. A homogeneous unit is a section of a society whose members have some definite characteristics in common. It may consist of a language group, an ethnic entity, an occupational level, or other sector of population with a strong feeling of "our group." Membership figures for homogeneous groups reveal which groups are more responsive to the Gospel.

The second body of facts needed relates to information about new members. Statistics on the number of baptisms for as many years as possible are highly significant. These figures are also needed for: the entire Church; each geographical, administrative or cultural area; every homogeneous unit; and every local church. Baptismal figures must also be refined.

Refining baptismal statistics consists of drawing a distinction between the baptism of children of members, (called *biological growth*) and the baptism or confirmation of adult believers, (called *conversion*

Getting the Facts of Growth

growth). A Church truly grows only by baptisms from the world (cf. McGavran, 1970:89-90). The number of new members transferring into the congregations, (called *transfer growth*), must also be clarified.

A third body of facts needed relates to other aspects of Church development. The stability of the Church's membership must be considered. Statistics on the number of members who leave the membership of the Church and how and why they leave are vital information. Facts about members who transferred to other Churches, who reverted to the world, who were excommunicated, or who died, must be compiled. These statistics, often among the most difficult to find, add significantly to the understanding of church growth.

A Church might consider itself to be growing rapidly because of large numbers entering by baptism. However, if research indicates almost equal numbers reverting to the world, the growth must be suspect. Thus, information on membership stability is necessary.

Factual information on the degree of faithfulness of members is needed. The number of members who actually attend the services of the churches and who take part in church activities is revealing. Some indication of the spiritual growth of Christians is instructive. The evangelistic activity and fruitfulness of members should be measured and recorded.

A great deal about Church growth is learned from information concerning numbers of congregations and workers, especially those sometimes called lay workers. Figures showing the number of congregations and workers, year by year, indicate the growth pattern. Statistics relating to the level of giving by the members must be ascertained and recorded.

Some information as to how the churches are developing in regard to teaching, training, and social ministries should be included. The number of members involved in systematic Bible study compared with total membership figures aids in understanding church development. The ability of the congregations to carry out the usual responsibilities of churches should be sought and reported.

The fourth body of facts needed relates to the indigeneity of the churches. The term indigenous church looms large in modern missionary language. The level of adaptation of the churches to the local culture is vital and the church's attainment of this adaptation must be evaluated. A technique for ascertaining indigeneity will be suggested.

The fifth body of facts needed relates to the families of the members. Family analysis lends important insights into Church growth. The degree to which members are inter-related reveals the lines along which the Gospel is spreading and the churches are growing. Information regarding the number of full families and the number of split families in the churches is most significant (cf. McGavran 1970: 92).

The sixth body of facts needed relates to the Church organization and the Mission organization. It is important to know for what purposes the personnel and funds of each organization are being used. Facts about plans and procedures of each organization must be known and described. If both organizations exist, there must be an understanding of projects and areas in which each is working independently and in which they are cooperating. The total working arrangement of the national organization and the mission organization must be set forth.

The seventh body of facts needed relates to workers. Statistics about the percentage of national

Getting the Facts of Growth 31

and missionary workers indicate if leadership is more national or missionary oriented. The numbers of ordained and unordained workers must be discovered. The increase or decrease in workers is important. Levels of education, schools attended, age, years of experience in the ministry, and years served at the present position reveal important facts about development. The primary type of ministry of each missionary should be clarified.

The attitudes of workers--both national and missionary--should be discovered and compared. In one country there was a controversy over unordained leaders presiding at the Lord's Supper. A comparison of national and missionary feelings was revealing. At times a comparison of attitudes between younger and older workers, between workers in geographical areas or types of work, and between workers of varying educational background is significant.

The foregoing represents a mountain of factual material. At first glance, one might be tempted to despair. Actually, the task of gathering these facts, while formidable, is not impossible.

FINDING THE NEEDED FACTS

The facts of growth are available; they are not, however, readily available. Finding the facts of growth is a sweaty and demanding, yet rewarding and revealing undertaking.

Statistical and historical records assist in finding the facts of growth. Records of membership totals, baptisms, numbers of congregations, workers, giving, assignment of personnel, and numerous other facts lay hidden and ready to be uncovered in Church and Mission records. Denominational reports usually include statistical summaries. Local churches often have yearly reports that reveal facts of growth.

A helpful technique at this stage of fact gathering is the construction of a table upon which data can be recorded as it is uncovered. This table then becomes a magnet to attract hard data and serves as the source of information on which later interpretation is based.

Books, articles, and letters provide facts. However, as one uses such sources, he must sift the true facts from promotional emphasis or biased views. Every writing that relates to the churches under study should be scrutinized to gain what *facts* it contains about church growth.

Sociological research techniques assist in finding the facts of growth. Church growth is a sociological phenomenon. As such, it can be studied through the scientific discipline of sociological research techniques.

Perhaps the best advice in regard to sociological techniques is, "get professional help." This manual does not attempt to give detailed instructions about samples, questionnaires, interview schedules, coding, statistics, or computer usage. However, since trained help is often unavailable, some guides in these techniques are included. More detailed suggestions are available in basic works on sociological research methods.*

---

*Among helpful books are: C. H. Backstrom and G. D. Hursh, *Survey Research*, (1963); W. J. Goode and P. K. Hatt, *Methods in Social Research*, (1952); Ralph Thomlinson, *Sociological Concepts and Research*, (1965); Pauline Young, *Scientific Social Surveys and Research*, (1966); Hubert M. Blalock, Jr., *An Introduction to Social Research*, (1970); N. M. Downie and R. W. Heath, *Basic Statistical Methods*, id. ed. (1970).

Getting The Facts of Growth

Sociological research methods are used to find the greatest amount of useful and reliable material with the available time and funds. A time-conserving technique is *random sampling*. Sampling, as the name implies, is a small representation of the larger whole (Goode and Hatt, 1952:209).

Social scientists have proved that conclusions based on properly derived random samples are equally as valid as conclusions based on the analysis of the entire group (Young 1966:326). However, a sample's reliability depends on its being representative. To insure representativeness, every person in the group must have an equal chance of being included in the sample. Size of the sample is less important than representative small sample than a non-representative large one" (Thomlinson, 1965:71).

The danger of bias in sampling was clearly revealed in one Church Growth Survey. Available statistics showed that only 1.8% of the members had ever been members of any other Church. Feeling that this figure was too low, the surveyors sought an explanation. They found that the figures available were from rural areas in which few other Church groups were working. When the figures from the city churches were included, the sample became more representative, and the more believable figure of 17% for transfer growth was obtained.

A representative study can be achieved by dividing the churches into groups and selecting a given number from each type. Some possible groupings might be: rural, 20-50 members; rural, 50-100 members; rural, 100-200 members; rural, over 200 members. Then, village and city churches can be likewise grouped. Other groups might include churches established less than five years, less than ten years, or more than ten years. Still other groups could be churches near universities and churches primarily among working people. Geographic considerations could easily constitute another group.

After the churches are grouped, some system of random selection should guide to which churches would actually be included from each group. *The main principle is insuring that every member (not church) in a given grouping has an equal chance of being included in the survey sample, unless it is the typical character of a church that is of interest. In that case, each church (not member) must be equally likely to be chosen.* See below.

After the churches to be sampled are isolated, some technique such as selecting every ninth or twelfth or 100th member on the membership rolls to receive questionnaires or to be interviewed can be employed.* If it seems important to get a cross section of age or sex differentials, then the Sunday School rolls might be used if these are divided by age and sex. Again, the principle that every member of a given group has equal chance to be selected must be observed.

Information from this sample, providing bias has been avoided, will be both accurate and reliable for the groups isolated. Facilities at the disposal of the researcher govern the size of the sample. Sampling allows more efficient use of the surveyor's time and effort.

---

*But note that if you select 30 to be interviewed or questioned in each grouping, you may only need to take one out of 20 or 50 or 100 where the grouping includes a large number of members. Sampling theory shows that a random sample of 30 out of 5,000 people is not significantly less accurate than 30 out of 500. In other words, a random sample is as accurate as its size not its size compared to or as a percentage of the population being sampled. A severe bias may enter in where people selected do not all answer and others who do take their place. Thus, randomness is lost if every entity randomly selected is not actually sampled.

One of the most useful research techniques for Church Growth Surveys is the *questionnaire*. Well-constructed questionnaires, used in conjunction with sampling techniques, provide volumes of reliable and accurate material. Questionnaires are designed to be answered by the respondent without any personal contact with an interviewer. They must, therefore, be absolutely clear.

Questionnaires uncover vast amounts of factual material, such as age, education, length of service, marital status, how long one has been a Christian, and attitudes on specific questions. The percentage of members, or workers, who hold certain positions can be found by using questionnaires.

Questions such as, "Were you ever a member of any other Church?" can be answered yes or no. However, it is more instructive to ask, "Before joining this Church were you a member of: 1) Baptist Church; 2) Methodist Church; 3) Presbyterian Church?" This question indicates not only the fact of transfer growth, but from what Churches the transferring had come.

Questionnaires reveal matters such as faithfulness. A question, "Do you attend mid-week service twice a month or more?" reveals the member's faithfulness to this service. A question concerning the year one was saved and his present position of service in the church reveals the spiritual progress made.

Unusual opportunities for comparison and correlation are provided through the use of questionnaires, particularly if computers are employed. For instance, by comparison techniques, it is possible to know what percentage of the pastors who studied in a particular school hold a certain theological position. Also, one could find what percentage of the members under a certain age have unsaved family members.

Surveys can use five types of questionnaires. A questionnaire for *church members* concentrates on finding vital statistics of members such as age, sex, marital status, educational level, and type of work. The questionnaires in one survey revealed that a large percentage of members were students in junior high school. The group understood the need of emphasizing student work among this age group more than among the more resistant college students.

The member questionnaire will answer questions such as who won the person to the Lord and when. Facts about faithfulness, service, and the religious situation in the person's home are revealed. Religious background can be ascertained with questions such as, "Before you became a Christian, what religion did you follow: 1) Islam; 2) Buddhism; 3) Hindu; 4) other?" The intensity with which one followed the former religion can be gauged by such questions as, "While a Muslim, did you attend the Mosque 1) once a month; 2) twice a month; 3) more often?" Questionnaires for members also reveal what influences led a member to Christ and to what degree he is active in witnessing.

Questionnaires reveal the level of the member's biblical knowledge. Should the questionnaire show that a large percentage of members are lacking in basic biblical knowledge, the group should move to correct this deficiency. Probably, it would be wise to use separate questionnaires to find general facts about members and their biblical knowledge.

Sampling techniques should be used in connection with questionnaires for church members. They allow the needed information to be secured with the least outlay of time and effort.

A questionnaire for *every local church* seeks the facts of growth for that congregation. Statistical

Getting the Facts of Growth

information on membership, baptisms, giving and activities over a period of years is requested. It compiles facts concerning the establishment of the church (i.e., who began the congregation, who was the first national pastor, etc.). The church's involvement in outreach, training ministry, its attainment of self-support, and other factors are investigated by this questionnaire. Facts such as services held, the pastor's salary, and the composition of the membership can all be found by the local church questionnaire.

As already mentioned, sampling techniques may be used with the local church questionnaire. But since churches are not as numerous as members, it is desirable to include all churches where possible. Information on the churches is among the most valuable gathered by the survey.

Another questionnaire seeks the age, educational background, place of training, length of time in the ministry, length of service at the present position, status of ordination, and many other facts about *pastors and workers*. Indications of attitude are also ascertained by the worker's questionnaire. Matters of relationships, theological and ecclesiological issues, and views toward evangelism are discovered through this questionnaire. Ideally, the worker's questionnaire is sent to all leaders, but if necessary, sampling can be used.

Every *institution* should receive a special questionnaire that will investigate how the objectives and efforts of the institution relate to church growth. This questionnaire seeks facts about support, policies, and overall effectiveness. The institutions are asked to indicate their plans for accomplishing the objectives of the group.

Finally, a questionnaire for *missionaries* determines the facts such as the missionary's age, training, and etc. Its main purpose would be to determine the degree of a missionary's effectiveness in achieving his objectives. It would seek to determine the reasons for success or failure. Questions such as, "How many people a missionary has won to the Lord in the past year" and "How many congregations the missionary has planted in a certain length of time," give light on the missionary's effectiveness. Germane to understanding why the missionary is successful are questions related to how he spends his time, what methods he follows, how he identifies with nationals, what problems he encounters in his work, his language proficiency, and his relationship to the local churches.

No attempt to provide sample questionnaires is made because each survey needs a special set of facts. No general questionnaire will suffice. We will, however, give a few tips on constructing questionnaires.

First, decide what facts you need to know and design the questionnaire to find them. Other questions no matter how interesting, should be dropped. This procedure keeps the questionnaire from being too long.

Second, be certain every question is clearly stated. One survey included a question, "How many people have you won to the Lord in the last year?" Some answered the question by stating how many had responded to invitations while they had been preaching. Since the intent of the question was how many had been won in personal witnessing, the lack of clarity lessened the accuracy of the material.

Third, construct tables for recording questionnaire results and consider how answers to questions will aid in understanding. This procedure will reveal if questions are valid or not. One survey included a question for missionaries as to what seminary they had attended. While the information was interesting, upon compiling the results of the questionnaires, it was plain that the information was not germane. The question could have been eliminated. Serious consideration to interpretive procedures before the questionnaire is circulated will increase the questionnaire's effectiveness.

Fourth, arrange items in the questionnaire logically. All questions relating to certain basic ideas should be arranged together. Begin with the easier questions and work toward the more difficult. Move smoothly from one subject to another. Careful arrangement can also avoid such embarrassments as occurred on a questionnaire that followed the question, "How many children do you have?" with, "Are you married?"

Fifth, state questions so as to minimize embarrassment or resentment. To ask, "Have you visited a medicine man since you became a Christian?" would probably illicit a negative answer regardless of the facts, due to embarrassment of admitting to the act. A more accurate response might be gained by asking, "Do you know Christians who visit medicine men?" Then follow with the question, "Do you feel they should?"

Sixth, the questionnaire should be tested before general use. Trying the questionnaire on a small group will reveal confusing and irrelevant questions. Testing will likely reveal the need of revision.

Seventh, be certain to express appreciation to the respondents. Questionnaires should begin with an explanation of the study and close with an expression of thanks.

Finally, there is value in using *computer technology* in conjunction with questionnaires (or other phases of the survey). Computer usage multiplies the value of the questionnaires. A computer readout from a "correlation analysis" may highlight relationships between variables which might otherwise be overlooked. This will reveal trends which would not be discovered by merely counting answers and noting totals. The computer also shows percentages, thus making implications of the information more understandable.

If the committee plans to use a computer, it should consult with a computer technician (preferably one who has some understanding of statistical methods) in the preparation of questionnaires. This will enable the committee to make maximum use of the computer at a minimum cost. Technical help at this point is indispensable.

These suggestions concerning questionnaires should provide some help. However, the reader is reminded that if possible, professional help is advisable.

Interviews are especially useful in Church Growth Surveys. Interviewing procedures give a flexibility not possible with questionnaires. Ideas can be followed up and a more adequate idea of attitudes and feelings gained.

Interviews, to be most effective, should employ an interview plan or schedule. In some cases the interview schedule is composed and used exactly as a questionnaire, the difference being that the interviewer records the responses. Obviously, this procedure limits the number of respondents who can be consulted.

The interview schedule can also be used as a guide for the interview. In this procedure, more "open-ended" questions can be used with the possibilities of uncovering other factors related to the central issues.

Getting the Facts of Growth 41

Whatever procedure is followed, definite plans should be made as to the use of the results of the interviews. The schedule should be constructed with usefulness of results in mind.

A rather involved, but helpful technique of social research, called *coding*, aids in classifying answers to open-ended questions. Open-ended questions, since they do not have definite choices or answers, produce variations in response. To classify these answers, categories or classes of answers are set up and given a symbol, usually numerical. For instance, a question on the missionary questionnaire (or schedule) might be, "What is your greatest frustration?" The answers might be coded as: (1) those related to living conditions; (2) those related to finances; (3) those related to children; (4) those related to relationships with nationals; (5) those related to relationships to missionaries; (6) those related to the work; (7) those related to a lack of fulfillment. Coding, since it provides a convenient method of classifying responses to questions with indefinite answers, has great usefulness in research.

Sociological research techniques materially contribute to Church Growth Surveys. These techniques allow the greatest accumulation of facts with the resources available. The techniques should be employed to the fullest extent possible.

INDIGENEITY SCALES

Indigeneity scales assist in finding the facts of growth. The indigenous church is one of the "in" words of modern ecclesiology. There has been, however, little help for empirically finding the level of indigeneity of a congregation or Church.

Traditionally the indigenous church (or Church) has been described in terms of the three selfs--self-supporting, self-governing, and self-propagating.

Charles Kraft indicates that a church might fulfill the three selfs and still fall short of being truly indigenous (1973:39). A. R. Tippett has added significantly to the understanding of the indigenous church (1969:134-36).

The survey must determine the level of indigeneity of each congregation in regard to each of these "marks" of indigeneity. Indigeneity scales provide empirical categories for gauging the level of indigeneity of any congregation or Church.

The indigeneity scales used here are: Self-adapting to local culture; self-functioning; self-supporting; self-determining; self-giving; and self-propagating. The principle of these scales is that churches (or Churches) are neither fully indigenous nor non-indigenous. Churches tend toward indigeneity. Scales of indigeneity reveal this tendency.

The scales of indigeneity are composed of five questions related to each of the six categories of indigeneity. With each question, certain indicators are given to aid the surveyor in rating the church's attainment in that category.

The church is rated from one to five on each question. A church scoring high in relation to a given question receives a rating of four or five. A church falling short of indigeneity in relation to a given question is rated two, one, or even zero. A congregation judged to be average in relation to some question is rated three.

After the church is rated on each question within a category, the surveyor adds the figures for the five questions. A church rated 4,3,3,4,3 for the five questions in the category, self-propagation for example, achieves a figure of 17. This figure

Getting the Facts of Growth 43

is plotted on a scale of indigeneity for that particular category. Such a scale appears below:

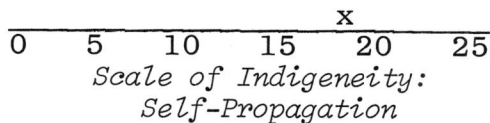
*Scale of Indigeneity:
Self-Propagation*

This church tends toward indigeneity in regard to self-propagation.

The six scales of indigeneity are given on the next pages. By carefully using these scales, surveyors can empirically gauge the level of indigeneity for a congregation in relation to each of the six categories.

SCALE OF INDIGENEITY: SELF-ADAPTING

1. ARE CHURCH ACTIVITIES CARRIED OUT IN THE LANGUAGE MOST FAMILIAR? _____
    If activities are in other than national or regional language, rate 0 or 1. If national language is used, but a regional language is more usual for the members, rate 2 or 3. If both national and regional languages are used or the language used is most common, rate 4 or 5.

2. IS THE MUSIC IN THE CHURCH ADAPTED TO THE CULTURE? _____
    If most hymns are translations and western instruments are primarily used, rate 1. If some hymns with local tunes and rhythms are used, rate 2,3, or 4. If many hymns have local sounds and extensive use is made of local instruments, rate 4 or 5.

3. ARE SERVICES CONDUCTED IN CULTURALLY APPROPRIATE WAYS? _____
    If times, ways, and order of worship are mostly patterned after Western ways, rate 1 or 2. If there is some adaptations (time, arrangement of seating, etc.), rate 2 or 3. If services are conducted in ways natural to the people, rate 4 or 5.

4. DO MEMBERS REMAIN IN DIRECT CONTACT WITH THEIR CULTURE AND FRIENDS? _____
    If church rules and ways make members appear foreign to non-Christians, rate 1 or 2. If members can fit into their culture but some local customs are prohibited *with no Christian substitutes*, rate 2 or 3. If there is much adaptation, rate 4 or 5.

Getting the Facts of Growth

5. IS THE MEMBERSHIP MOSTLY FROM ONE HOMOGENEOUS GROUP?
   If membership is extensively mixed racially or socially, rate 1 or 2. If membership is evenly divided between groups, rate 3. If membership is primarily from one homogeneous group, rate 4 or 5.

                                        Total ____

   ```
   0    5    10   15   20   25
   ```
   Scale of Indigeneity
   Self-Adapting

* *

SCALE OF INDIGENEITY: SELF-SUPPORTING

1. DOES MEMBER-GIVING SUPPORT ALL THE CHURCH'S BUDGET NEEDS?
   If subsidy is needed for church to meet budget expenses, rate 1 or 2, according to percentages. If one-half or more of support is by member giving, rate 3 or 4. If no subsidy is needed, rate 5.

2. DOES CHURCH FULFILL ALL ITS FINANCIAL OBLIGATIONS BY MEMBER-GIVING?
   If all needs are met, rate 4 or 5. If some financial needs are not met on a regular basis (repayment of loans, gifts to association, social ministry), rate accordingly, 3, or 2, or 1.

3. DOES/DID THE CHURCH PROVIDE ITS OWN PLACE OF WORSHIP?
   If the place of worship was provided without aid, rate 5. If the church was aided in the provision of the place of worship, rate according

to local participation in the provision, 4,3,2, or 1.

4. DOES THE CHURCH MAINTAIN ITS OWN PLACE OF WORSHIP? _____
If the meeting place is adequately maintained by the church, rate 5. If subsidy is needed for maintenance, rate 1 or 2. If the church receives no aid for upkeep but the meeting place is inadequately maintained, rate 1 or 2. If church assumes most responsibility for maintenance, rate 3 or 4.

5. DOES THE CHURCH GIVE REGULARLY FOR MISSIONARY AND SOCIAL CAUSES? _____
If 10% or more of church income is given for missionary and social causes, rate 5. if less, rate accordingly.

Total _____

```
0    5    10   15   20   25
```
Scale of Indigeneity
Self-Supporting

* *

SCALE OF INDIGENEITY: SELF-GIVING

1. DOES THE CHURCH HAVE A PLAN FOR SOCIAL MINISTRY? _____
If a plan is fuctioning regularly, rate 4 or 5 depending on results. For irregular plan rate 2 or 3. For seldom used plan rate 1 or 2. If there is no plan, rate 0.

2. DOES THE CHURCH PARTICIPATE IN GOVERNMENT-PROMOTED PROGRAMS? _____

Getting the Facts of Growth

If church participates in most government-promoted programs (national and local) that are suitable for church participation, rate 4 or 5. If only occasionally, rate 2 or 3. If the church seldom or never participates, rate 1 or 0.

3. DOES THE CHURCH AID VICTIMS OF DISASTERS OTHER THAN MEMBERS? _____
   If there is a program to aid other than members, rate 3,4,5 according to how it is used. If the plan is often neglected, rate 2 or 3. If there is no plan or it is seldom, if ever, used, rate 0 or 1.

4. DOES THE CHURCH EMPHASIZE CHRISTIAN CITIZENSHIP? _____
   If some definite emphasis on Christian citizenship has been held in the last two years, rate 4 or 5 depending on attendance. If the last emphasis on citizenship was more than two years ago, rate 1,2, or 3. If there has never been emphasis on citizenship, rate 0.

5. DOES THE CHURCH SUPPORT DENOMINATIONAL SOCIAL MINISTRIES? _____
   If most denominational emphases are supported, rate 4 or 5. If these emphases are not well supported, rate 1,2, or 3 according to support.

                                    Total _____

```
  0    5    10   15   20   25
```
Scale of Indigeneity
Self-Giving

* *

SCALE OF INDIGENEITY: SELF-DETERMINING

1. ARE CHURCH DECISIONS REACHED BY PATTERNS APPROPRIATE TO THE SOCIETY? _____
   If the pattern of church government is foreign to the society, rate 1 or 2. If the pattern is basically adapted to the local culture rate 3 or 4. If church government is almost fully in line with local patterns, rate 5.

2. ARE LOCAL CONGREGATIONS FREE FROM MISSION CONTROL? _____
   If the Mission or missionaries control the local church, rate 0 or 1. If the church is free of mission control but missionaries exercise indirect control, rate 2 or 3. If the church is free of mission control or missionary control, rate 4 or 5.

3. IS THE LOCAL CONGREGATION FREE FROM CONTROL OF THE CENTRAL CHURCH ORGANIZATION? _____
   If the central organization has power over the local church, assigning pastors, demanding funds, approving ordination, etc., rate 1,2, or 3. If the central organization has only limited control over local churches, rate 3 or 4. If the church is basically free, rate 4 or 5.

4. DOES THE CHURCH HANDLE PROBLEMS OF DISCIPLINE? _____
   If outside power (mission, missionary, Church organization) assumes the responsibility for discipline, rate 1 or 2. If the church assumes this responsibility, rate 4 or 5. If the church has the responsibility but often ignores matters calling for discipline, rate 2 or 3.

Getting the Facts of Growth 49

5. ARE MEMBERS INVOLVED IN THE CHURCH DECISIONS?
If the leader (pastor or others) or some small group make decisions without consulting members, rate 1 or 2. If members have some voice, rate 3,4 or 5.

                                          Total _____

```
  0    5   10   15   20   25
```
Scale of Indigeneity
Self-Determining

* *

SCALE OF INDIGENEITY: SELF-FUNCTIONING

1. CAN LOCAL MEMBERS FILL ALL POSITIONS OF LEADERSHIP IN THE CHURCH?
If many positions must be filled by other than local members, rate 1 or 2. If most positions can be filled by local members (even if they are now filled by other than local members), rate 3. If all or almost all positions can and are filled by local members, rate 4 or 5.

2. IS THERE A PROGRAM OF LEADERSHIP TRAINING FOR THE CHURCH?
If there is a continuous training program and some members are training, rate 4 or 5. If the training program is irregular or few are now in training, rate 3 or 2. If the training program is seldom used or does not exist, rate 1 or 0.

3. ARE LAYMEN ACTIVE IN THE SERVICE OF THE CHURCH?
If laymen are used in every level of leadership (baptizing, leading church ordinances, etc.), rate 5. If laymen are used but in

limited roles, rate 4 or 3 according to use.
If laymen are primarily observers and the
work of the church is in the hands of the
professional clergy, rate 1.

4. DO MEMBERS ASSUME RESPONSIBILITY FOR CHURCH
   PROBLEMS? _____
   If members turn to missionaries and pastors
   when problems arise (such as financial,
   moral, threats, etc.) rate 1, 2, or 3.
   If the members themselves take responsibility for church problems, rate 3,4, or
   5 depending on the level of responsibility.

5. DOES THE CHURCH HELP MEMBERS WHO SUFFER
   MISFORTUNE? _____
   If this ministry is regular and well-
   administered, rate 4 or 5. If it often
   neglected or seldom carried out, rate 1,
   2, or 3.

                                    Total _____

```
   0     5    10    15    20    25
```
Scale of Indigeneity
Self-Functioning

* *

SCALE OF INDIGENEITY:
SELF-PROPAGATING

1. DOES THE CHURCH HAVE MISSION POINTS OR
   EVANGELISTIC POSTS? _____
   If there is a mission or evangelistic post
   for every 25 members, rate 5. If there is
   one for every 50 members, rate 4. If there
   is one for every 100 members, rate 3. If
   there is one for every 200 members, rate 2.
   If there is a plan for a mission but it has
   not yet started and there are no other

Getting the Facts of Growth

missions, rate 1. If there are no missions or evangelistic posts and none are planned, rate 0.

2. HAS THE CHURCH STARTED A NEW MISSION OR EVANGELISTIC POINT IN THE LAST TWO YEARS? _____
If the answer is yes, rate 5. If the last post was started three or four years ago, rate 4. If the last post was started more than five years ago, rate 3. If the last point was more than eight years ago, rate 2. If the church has not started a point in the last ten years, rate 1. If never, rate 0.

3. HAS THE CHURCH HELD A SOUL-WINNING COURSE FOR MEMBERS? _____
If course was held in the last three years, rate 4 or 5 depending on the attendance. If the course was five years ago, rate 2 or 3. If longer than five years ago, rate 1. If no such course has been held, rate 0.

4. ARE MISSION POINTS SHEPHERDED BY MEMBERS OF THE CHURCH? _____
If members work in the mission points, rate 4 or 5. If only the pastor and/or students from the training school work in the points, rate 2 or 3. If members seldom serve in the mission points, rate 1.

5. DID THE CHURCH BAPTIZE ONE NEW MEMBER FOR EACH EIGHT MEMBERS LAST YEAR? _____
If answer is yes, rate 5. If one was baptized for each 15 members, rate 4. If the record was one baptism for every 30 members, rate 3. If it was one for every 60 rate 2. If less, rate 1. If there were no baptisms, rate 0.

Total _____

```
  0    5   10   15   20   25
```
Scale of Indigeneity
Self-Propagating

* *

After the Church has been rated for each of the six categories, the results of these ratings are averaged. For example, a Church rated 10 in relation to self-adapting, self-determining, 5 for self-giving, and 5 for self-propagating, achieves an overall average of 9. This result is plotted on a comprehensive scale of indigeneity, as shown below:

```
           x
  0    5   10   15   20   25
```
Comprehensive
Scale of Indigeneity

Overall, this church tends toward non-indigeneity.

Obviously, a high level of subjectivity is involved in ratings on the scales of indigeneity. This subjectivity cannot be totally avoided. It can be greatly reduced by asking three different persons to independently rate the churches. Then the average rating of the three persons is accepted as the indicator for the level of indigeneity of the church.

The scales of indigeneity are designed primarily for local churches. They can be easily adapted, however, to the study of an entire Church or other group of churches.

One procedure for using the scales of indigeneity for a Church or group of churches is as follows.*

---

*Also, a frequency distribution (see next chapter) can be plotted.

Getting the Facts of Growth

Add and average the ratings of every church *on each question in all six categories*. For example, a group of eight churches received ratings of 2,4,3,2,3,3,3, and 4 on the first question of the category self-adapting. The sum (24) divided by the number of churches (8) produced an average of 3. This figure, together with the like averages from each of the other four questions in the category was used to construct a scale of indigeneity in relation to self-adapting.

Repeat this procedure for each of the six categories. The figures from each category are then used to formulate a comprehensive scale of indigeneity for the group. For example, the eight churches above found that they achieve a rating of 15 for self-adapting, 10 for self-functioning, 10 for self-supporting, 15 for self-determining, 20 for self-giving and 20 for self-propagating. These figures produced an average of 15. Plotted on a comprehensive scale of indigeneity, this figure revealed a scale as seen below:

$$\begin{array}{cccccc} & & & x & & \\ \hline 0 & 5 & 10 & 15 & 20 & 25 \end{array}$$

Comprehensive Scale of Indigeneity

This Church tends toward indigeneity.

The scales of indigeneity indicate not only the level of indigeneity of the church (or Church) but the exact point at which the group needs to move closer to the ideal of indigeneity. If a group finds it ranks low in regard to self-functioning, the group must seek to improve its self-functioning ability. Furthermore, by noticing upon which of the five questions in a given category it scores low, the group can ascertain exactly the areas where concentration is demanded.

CONCLUSION

Getting the facts of growth obviously is not an easy matter. Through the use of historical and statistical records, sociological research techniques, and the scales of indigeneity, the survey can uncover the facts of growth. Having found these facts, the survey proceeds to objectify them so that they can be more effectively studied and interpreted.

5
Objectifying the Facts of Growth

The facts obtained from statistics, questionnaires, and interviews must be visualized, or shall we say objectified. The importance of visualizing the facts clearly, accurately, and strikingly cannot be overemphasized, for interpretation and evaluation are sharpened when the facts stand before you in simple, understandable forms. We will consider several techniques for objectifying the facts of growth: simple graphs of growth, average annual growth rate, graphs of rates of growth (semi-logarithmic graphs), percentages, ratios, distributions, and comparative analysis of growth.

DRAWING SIMPLE GRAPHS OF GROWTH

Church growth research relies heavily on graphs of growth showing membership at various points over a period of time. No other technique is so productive in objectifying church growth materials. Concerning the value of such graphs, McGavran observes:

> Columns of figures giving the membership of any church and its homogeneous units contain locked-up knowledge. By careful study the figures can be forced to reveal their secrets, but the process is tedious. When, however, each set of figures is transformed into a graph of growth,

the secrets leap out at the reader. He who would
understand church growth should construct line
graphs showing at a glance what has transpired.
He can then ask why it happened (1970:108).

The process of graph construction can be relatively simple. Using graph paper (or other surface divided carefully), construct a horizontal scale representing the years of the church's (or congregation's) existence. Construct a vertical scale on which the number of members year by year can be plotted. Indicate the membership by placing a dot on the graph according to the membership each year. A picture of the growth of the church appears in the form of a line graph when the dots representing membership are joined. Since Vergil Gerber's little book, *God's Way to Keep a Church Going and Growing*, is an assumed possession for readers of this book, simple graphs and semi-logarithmic graphs are discussed (Gerber, 1973). We will treat the latter further on in this chapter.

Ideally, there will be a membership figure for each year. Practically, it is often not possible to attain such complete statistical information. Even when forced to use membership figures for intervals of three to five years, a valuable picture of growth is obtained. It is wise to draw dotted lines between points when a year or more is missing in between points of known data, since you may otherwise overlook the possibility of major variations in the intervening period. Helpful suggestions on drawing graphs can be seen in McGavran, *Understanding Church Growth*, pp. 121-22.

Graphs should be constructed for each region or type of work--that is, one graph should be constructed for each province, district, or administrative area and all homogeneous units being studied, as well as for each type of work being carried out (such as street evangelism, door-to-door evangelism, medical clinics, etc...). For comparative purposes, it is

Objectifying the Facts of Growth

quite useful when all regional graphs are constructed on the same scale. For example, Roy Shearer's study of the growth of the Presbyterian Church in Korea has been mentioned as an outstanding example of the value of regional comparisons. Shearer's graphs of each of the nine presbyteries indicated that the Church had been growing chiefly in the two northern presbyteries and there had not been a general movement over the entire area (1966:82-83).

Graphs should also be constructed for as many of the local congregations as possible, again, all on the same scale to facilitate comparisons. For even more striking comparisons, the membership graphs of several churches can be plotted on the same paper as well.

But graphs can also picture other types of factual information, such as records of baptisms, giving, number of congregations, etc., so that comparisons of factors in *one* church, such as its membership and baptisms, can also be objectified when plotted on the same sheet (cf. McGavran, 1970:90). Care should be taken, however, not to create a confusing picture by including too much material on any one graph.

Besides line graphs, there are also other kinds of graphs that can be utilized. Bar graphs, for example (see Table VI, Figure 4 on page 75), and pie graphs can often show percentage material and comparative material in spectacular fashion. The survey should seek every way possible and practical to construct graphs to help visualize the facts of growth, thereby providing a sound basis for analysis and interpretation.

In summary, the phenomenon of growth is time-related, so the horizontal dimension in your graphs will be time, usually years. The vertical scale will usually be membership, attendance, number of baptisms from the world (i.e. not counting children brought up in the church), or baptisms of members' children,

Bibles brought to church, verses memorized, number of small weekly prayer meetings - whatever you would like to trace. A glance at such a graph will tell you any irregularity, and that, in turn, will set off other questions to explore. However, there are some things that need to be calculated as well as graphed.

CALCULATING GROWTH RATES

To objectify growth or non-growth on a simple line graph is important. Many times this step alone, however, clouds as much as it reveals. For example, as a church gets bigger its membership base gets bigger and it will be misleading to compare its yearly increase in a later period with that of an earlier period if the comparison is based simply on the number of new members added. A 50 member jump on the graph in an early period when a church has only 100 members is much more significant than if the church has a 1,000 membership and grows by 50. Yet on ordinary graph paper the line on the graph only moves up the same amount. This is why simple line graphs of membership often get steeper as the years go past even though the growth (in proportion to membership) may get relatively smaller, as it often does when congregations and denominations get older and larger. Therefore, the most revealing question to ask in regard to comparative growth rates is a question of the percentage rate of growth, i.e.: "How many new members are there at the end of a given period, for every hundred who were already members?" Or, simply, "how many new members (baptisms, or converts from the world, etc.) per hundred former members?"

For example, a net increase of 10 members starting with 100 is, by such a measurement, just as good as a net increase of 40 starting with 400, or 25 starting with 250. In each case you divide the net increase by how many hundred members there are at the beginning of the period (e.g. 10 ÷ 1, 40 ÷ 4, 25 ÷ 2.5 all equal 10).

Objectifying the Facts of Growth

Now, of course, raw data rarely comes in the nice round numbers of our examples. The following cases of growth during a single year are more typical:

TABLE I

	A Beginning Membership	B Ending Membership	C Net Increase (B-A)	D Beginning Members ÷ by 100, (A÷100)	E Calculation (C÷D)	Answer: New members per 100 (=% increase)
1.	400	440	40	4.00	40÷4	10 %
2.	420	483	63	4.20	63÷4.2	15 %
3.	285	410	125	2.85	125÷2.85	43.8%
4.	1,260	1,640	380	12.60	380÷12.60	30.2%
5.	30,400	32,500	2,100	304.00	2,100÷304.00	6.9%

It is fascinating to note how the fastest growing church above is the one that added 43.8 (almost 44) new people for every hundred it started with (note this is 43.8%). You could not have seen this so easily by looking at the first two columns! Now you can see that bringing church growth facts fully into view requires the additional step of calculating the *rate* at which the church is growing.

However, in the example above we have assumed, for simplicity, that all of these Christian groups grew from size A to size B in the same length of time. The results as a percentage increase would not have been comparable had the periods been different lengths. That is, growing by 43.8% is *not* faster than 20% if the 20% took place in one year and the 43.8% took place in two years--or is it? Let's try to find out:

```
100   starting membership
 20   plus 20 more, i.e. add 20% of 100
120   end of first year
 24   plus 24 more, i.e. add 20% of 120
144   end of second year, or 44 more members in
         2 years
```

This answers the question above. A 20% growth rate per year over a two year period produced an increase of 44 new members per 100 original members or a growth of 44% per two years. This is faster than a growth rate of 43.8% per two years! That's right, a growth rate of 43.8% per two years is *not* faster than a growth rate of 20% per year.

Let's work at another example. Let's see what happens to a church with a growth rate of 10% per year over a period of 4 years. Each 100 members should grow as follows:

```
100
 10     plus 10 more, i.e. add 10% of 100
110     end of first year
 11     plus 11 more, i.e. add 10% of 110
121     end of second year
 12     plus 12 more, i.e. add 10% of 121
133     end of third year
 13     plus 13 more, i.e. add 10% of 133
146     end of fourth year or 46 more in 4 years
```

At this point, two additional observations are appropriate:

(1) Forty-six more per 100 in 4 years is a growth of 46% per 4 years. This is the result of adding 10% each year *NOT* 46÷4=11.5%! As in the first example, (which was 44 more in two years with a twenty per cent per year growth rate), *the average yearly increase cannot be computed by simply dividing the total increase by the number of years!*

(2) Likewise, since the average yearly percentage increase is what we call the average annual growth rate, it is equally wrong to calculate the latter (the AAGR) by dividing the increase per hundred members by the length of the period.

Let us summarize what we've just covered: *How to calculate percentage increase* (See Table I). You

Objectifying the Facts of Growth 61

divide the beginning membership (Col. A) by 100 to find how many groups of a hundred there are (Col. D). You can do this by moving the decimal point over to the left two digits. Then you divide that number into the net increase in membership (Col. C). The answer is the number of *net additional persons per starting hundred* (Col. F). This number is always equal to the percentage increase. Such percentages may be validly compared between any two sizes of churches (different churches or the same church at an earlier and later date) *just so long as the period during which the growth takes place is the same*. It takes one further step to compare what happens in periods of two different lengths. For this, we need to calculate the average growth rate per year (the AAGR) in order to make a meaningful comparison. We will consider this in the next section.

CALCULATING AVERAGE ANNUAL GROWTH RATE (AAGR)

Before considering further how to calculate the AAGR, let's look at another reason why the AAGR is so meaningful. Population growth rates, a measure of the biological growth of a nation, are generally given in terms of percent increase per year--what we call Average Annual Growth Rate! So, knowing the AAGR of a church let us compare it to population growth rates to see whether it is simply growing at a biological rate, or beyond.

For example, biological growth rates vary from near zero in developed countries to 3% or more in the developing nations. Here are some examples from the latest Population Reference Bureau Chart:

    Japan   1.3%   Libya   3.0%
    Germany   .3%   Nigeria 2.7%
    United Kingdom .3%   Brazil   2.8%
    USA   .9%   India   2.4%

What does this mean? It means that if a church in a developing nation grows only 3% per year, it may be no more than a biologically active younger community. Another example: one investigator was "amazed" that his Church had grown from 30,000 to 300,000 in 75 years, only to discover that its average annual growth rate had only been slightly more than 3%--the average annual population growth rate in his area!

Let's summarize the need for knowing the Average Annual Growth Rate:

First, from the previous section, it lets us meaningfully compare the growth of a church during two different periods of differing lengths.

Secondly, it lets us meaningfully compare the growth of different churches at different times over differing periods.

Thirdly, as we have just seen above, it lets us compare the growth of the church to its own biological growth and that of the community surrounding it.

How do you calculate the Average Annual Growth Rate?

First, you calculate the percentage increase without regard to the duration of the period. This we do in Column F as previously in the Table I. See Table II.

TABLE II

	A	B	C	D	E	F	G	H
1.	1238	3860	2592	12.68	2592÷12.68	204%	8 yrs	15
2.	3860	6082	2222	38.6	2222÷38.6	58%	5 yrs	10
3.	305	650	345	3.05	345÷3.05	113%	5 yrs	16
4.	30000	300000	270000	300	270000÷300	900%	75yrs	3

A=Beginning Membership
B=Ending Membership

C=Net Increase (B-A)
D=Beginning Members ÷ by 100, (A÷100)

E=Calculation (C÷D)
F=Answer: New members per 100 (% increase)
G=Length of Time

H=AAGR

Objectifying the Facts of Growth 63

The additions to Table I are the length or duration of the period (Col. G) and the Average Annual Growth Rate (Col. H). The duration of the period we know. But where did we get the Average Annual Growth Rate (AAGR)? See Table I in Appendix A on p. 117

There in Table I (Appendix A), we have calculated the AAGR for several periods (indicated across the top row of the table). To find the AAGR for your church, simply find the percentage increase (derived in Col. F of Table II) in the left hand column and run across to the number of years (top row) of the period. When the row and column intersect, you find the AAGR. In some cases you will not be able to find the exact percentage increase (as derived in Col. F of Table II) in the left column. In that case, you may have to "read between the lines" but you can come close enough for our purposes.

At least three other methods of calculating AAGR are available. C. P. Wagner's "Guidelines for Making Church Growth Calculations" is designed to do the calculations using a special calculator. Page 419 ff. in *The Means of World Evangelization*, edited by Alvin Martin, discusses the use of the slide rule and special logarithmic paper.

Some readers may still wonder why we can't just divide the eight year percentage increase of 204% (first example in Table II) by eight years to get the AAGR. According to this method, 204÷8 would give 25½%, not the figure of 15% on the chart. The quotient of 25½% above is the answer to a *different* question, namely: How many new members per year did each of the *original* members bring in? This would mean that new members since have had no part in sharing the faith, and that the people of the original congregation were the *only* ones causing it to grow.) This is therefore an unrealistic question to ask. The more meaningful question is the AAGR, that is, "How many people per year has each member brought in?," and this question can only be

answered by using the table in Appendix A (where the
calculations have already been made) or by the other
means referred to above.

It is almost inevitable, of course, that as any
church movement gets larger and older its very success tends to seal off its members (especially the
second and third generations) from evangelistic contact with non-Christian friends and relatives, thus
"the annual number of additional members per 100
existing members" tends to decrease. That is, the
AAGR tends to get smaller with time and size, even
though the momentum and popularity of a large church
tend to increase growth rates. Regardless of this,
knowing the AAGR makes comparisons with known biological growth for the general population meaningful
permits comparisons with other churches. All told,
it is probably the best single measure of growth
rate.

DRAWING GRAPHS OF GROWTH RATES

The next step of drawing graphs that show rates
of growth is actually easier and much faster to do
than the last step of making calculations. It is
easier because of the special tool called semi-logarithmic graph paper, which is used because its
vertical scale increases the way churches actually
grow. The power of this paper lies in the fact that
the growth of a church or biological community growing at a steady rate will be represented by a straight
line, whereas on a simple graph it will be a rapidly
steepening curve, even though the growth rate is constant. The steepness of the line on semi-logarithmic
paper is proportional to the *rate of growth*. This is
further illustrated in Gerber's book which shows why
it is a valuable tool and how easy it is to use it.
But if you do not have easy access to such graph
paper, you will be happy to know that you can make
it yourself. Directions for constructing it are
given further on in the chapter.

Objectifying the Facts of Growth

Semi-logarithmic paper is much easier to use than to explain. But for those who are interested in what it is, let us point out that the only difference between regular graph paper and semi-log paper is the vertical scale. Both kinds of paper have a horizontal axis that represents *years*. And for both, the vertical axis is *size*—size of membership, baptisms, attendance, or anything else. The difference is that the simple graph measures the vertical with a "linear" or "scalar" measure, while the semi-log paper measures the vertical with a special scale called "logarithmic." (The paper is called *semi*-logarithmic because only *one* of the scales is logarithmic.) The scale could also be called "digital," actually, because each "cycle" or major division increases by one digit. The first cycle starts with *one* (not zero). The second cycle adds a zero—beginning with 10. The third adds another zero, beginning with 100, etc. Or, if the first cycle is to begin with, say, 100, the second must add a zero—beginning with 1000, etc. [You can also see that the cycles are increasing exponentially. Because our number system is in Base 10, we are increasing each cycle by a power of 10: 10^0 (or 1), 10^1 (or 10), 10^2 (or 100), 10^3 (or 1,000), and so on. The exponent "2" in the expression "10^2" is the logarithm of 100 to the Base 10; hence the term "logarithmic" in "semi-logarithmic paper."]

The above is a brief explanation of semi-logarithmic paper, which is necessary to use in order to plot a clear picture of *growth rates*. If you cannot readily procure logarithmic graph paper, it is perfectly possible to construct your own with the measurements in the following table (see Table III). All you do is take a piece of 8½ x 11" blank paper and draw a horizontal line across the bottom (8½") of the paper, ½" up from the edge. Secondly you draw a vertical line up along the left edge, 3/4" from the edge. Now, on this vertical line, measuring from the bottom line, you mark off 6.35 centimeters, 12.70 centimeters, 19.05 centimeters and 25.40 centimeters. These are the four cycles. Now, the intermediate points are

also given in the table below. For the horizontal
scale, always use one inch for ten years, so that
all your charts will have equivalent meaning in curve
steepness, etc. (Figure I on page 68 is our own
example of semi-log paper with four cycles.)

TABLE III

Four Cycle Semi-Log Paper Measurements

Vertical   Distance in Centimeters Measured up from
Number   bottom

Cycle 1		Cycle 2		Cycle 3	
1	0.0	10	6.35	100	12.70
2	1.91	20	8.25	200	14.61
3	3.02	30	9.38	300	15.73
4	3.82	40	10.17	400	16.52
5	4.44	50	10.79	500	17.14
6	4.94	60	11.29	600	17.64
7	5.37	70	11.72	700	18.07
8	5.73	80	12.08	800	18.43
9	6.06	90	12.41	900	18.76

Cycle 4		Cycle 5	
1,000	19.05	10,000	25.40
2,000	20.96		
3,000	22.08		
4,000	22.87		
5,000	23.49		
6,000	23.99		
7,000	24.42		
8,000	24.78		
9,000	25.40		

Remember that a straight line drawn at any angle
on semi-logarithmic graph paper represents a constant
rate of growth. See the straight line in the graph
on p. 68 depicting a biological growth rate of 3%.

Objectifying the Facts of Growth

The steepness of the curved line at any point is in proportion to the rate of growth at that point. As the angle gets flatter, the rate is slower. The graph in Figure 1 is based upon Table IV, showing data on the Baptist Christian Community in Southern Mizoram (Northeast India). Notice how little knowledge one gets just by looking at the table. Only by objectifying these data do we begin to notice the significant facts of growth.

Table IV

Year	Community Membership	Year	Community Membership	Year	Community Membership
1902	45	1918	3,630	1934	15,980
1904	125	1920	4,790	1936	18,334
1906	304	1922	7,820	1938	19,343
1908	500	1924	8,770	1940	21,084
1910	805	1926	9,720	1944	23,108
1912	1,544	1928	10,031	1946	27,356
1914	2,739	1930	11,209	1954	37,760
1916	2,686	1932	13,380	1956	38,183
				1960	44,303

Figure 1 was drawn on four cycle semi-logarithmic paper similar to that described in Table III. Yearly changes in the AAGR for the community are indicated by the changing slope of the curved line. It is easy to see that the community has hardly grown more than biologically since 1944. This is readily seen by comparing its growth to a biological growth of 3% per year starting at 1944. This is shown by the straight line in Figure 1. During this period the AAGR for the community was 4.1%.

Now for a surprise. Look at Figure 2 on p. 69. There we see what appears to be a growing community. It is a community which is definitely growing and

FIGURE 1

Semi-logarithmic Graph of Growth of Southern Mizoram Baptist Christian Community from 1900 to 1960.

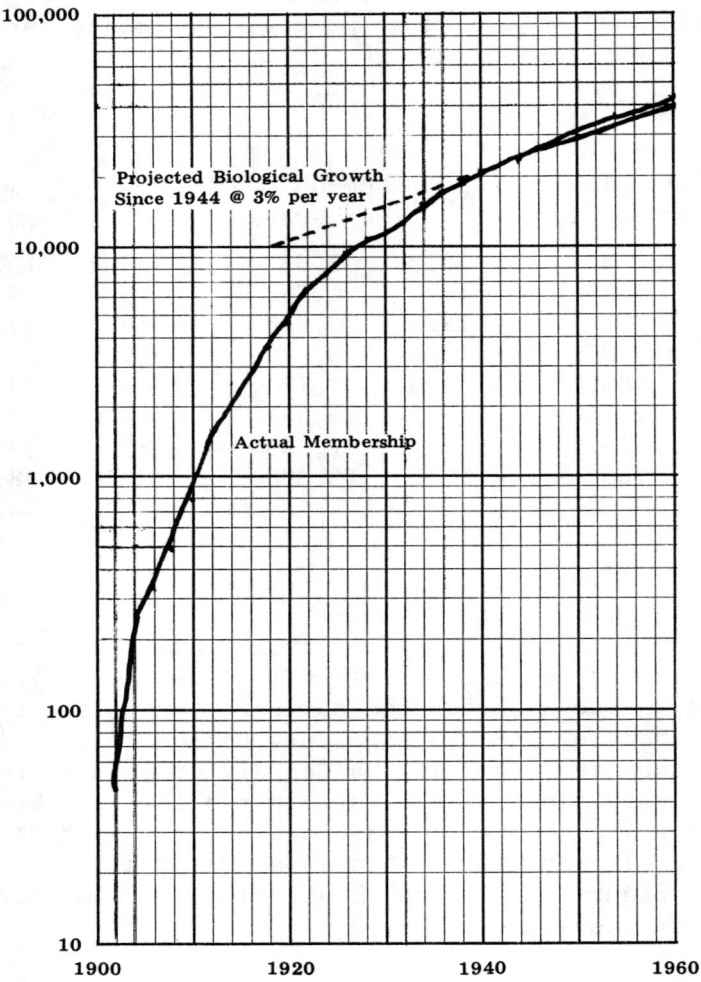

FIGURE 2

Arithmetic graph of growth of Southern Mizoram Baptist Christian Community from 1900 to 1960.

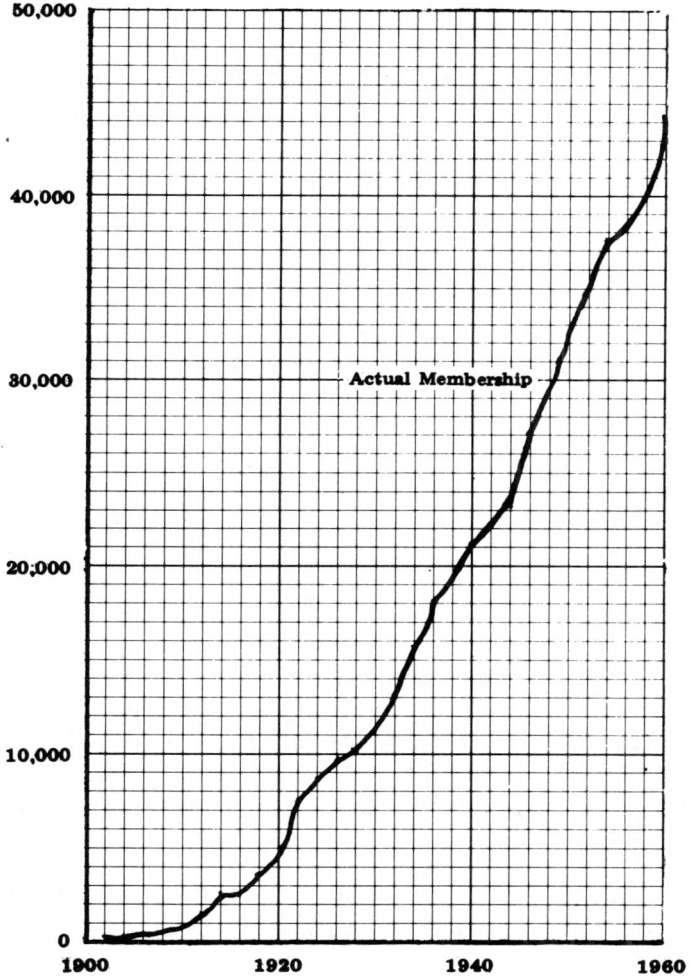

expanding -- *biologically!* It is exactly the same
community as depicted in Figure 1! What is the
difference? Figure 2 is a simple arithmetic plot.
This should amply demonstrate the worth of the little
extra effort required of the church diagnostician to
use and interpret graphs showing *rates* of church
growth as well as simple yearly membership graphs.
Now we are ready to go on to the next section dealing
with calculating precentages, rations, and distributions

CALCULATING PERCENTAGES, RATIOS, AND DISTRIBUTIONS

Percentages. Much factual material uncovered by
the survey can be objectified simply by calculating
percentages. The fact that 42% of the membership of
one church was "transfer growth" led to a renovation
of strategy. When another church learned that 81%
of its members lived within two kilometers of the
church they attended, the church recognized the need
to multiply the number of congregations. When 23%
of the missionaries in one survey reported having
won no one to Christ in an entire year, the group
was shocked into action. A great soul-winning field
was revealed by a survey that showed that 68% of the
church members were from non-Christian homes.

Just a note of caution: The way percentages are
presented can bias interpretation. One can say,
"Fifteen percent of the membership is a result of
transfer growth". Or he can say, "Eighty-five percent of the members have never been members of any
other church". Both statements may be made about
the same data. However, a different feeling is produced by the differing statements. This demonstrates
that we must be careful to project an accurate picture
when presenting statistical material.

Ratios. Ratios are also helpful. Knowing a given
church movement has grown to 24,000 members is further
illuminated by finding the average size of each congregation, that is, the ratio of total members of the
movement to regularly worshipping congregations. For

example, 24,000 members could be a single "congregation" in Chile. Or, it could be the aggregate of 200 congregations, in which case the average size would be 12 members per congregation. More common is 50 members on an average. Information of this type, if very large or very small, may signal the fact that a different definition of worshipping unit is being used. Another valuable ratio is the number of worshipping units per ordained or trained pastor. This may throw light on a training gap or an ordination lag, or both. Along this line it is valuable to learn the ratio of full members to trained pastors. How can a church be healthy and stable if there are many more than 50 or 100 full members per trained leader? McGavran, in fact, points out five kinds of leaders and the crucial relation between the ratios of these people (Arn and McGavran 1973:89-97). We need to ask questions such as: What is the ratio of class four to class one leaders etc?

Distributions. However, some factual material is not adequately objectified by percentages and ratios alone. Averages and frequency distributions may be useful in portraying facts which are otherwise obscure. For example, to know that 60% of the members are under 25 years of age is helpful, but to know that the average age is 21 may be still more helpful. In the same way a frequency distribution may be used to portray the exact breakdown of ages within the congregation.

Averages. Averages are computed by adding up all of the pieces of data and dividing by the number of pieces of data. It's that simple. For example, suppose there are five men in a Bible class, ages 18, 23, 26, 24, 24. The total of the data is 18+23+26+24+24=115. The average is 115 divided by 5 pieces of data to equal an average age of 23.

Frequency Distributions. Frequency distributions divide the data into groups called "class-intervals". The number of pieces of data in each group or class interval are tabulated and plotted to produce a "frequency distribution." Frequency distributions are primarily used to represent data which is continuous and quantifiable (i.e. representable by a number). This includes age, income, age at time of membership, social status (rated on a numerical scale from the highest, say 10, to the lowest) and so on.

How does it work? First, find out what the "range" is--the upper and lower limits of the data. For example, the age of members in a church may vary from a lower limit of ten to a maximum of seventy-one. Compute the range (or spread) of the data by subtracting the lower limit from the upper limit. (In this case 71 - 10 = 61.)

Second, choose a class-interval. The class interval is the width of the groups or categories we want to partition the data into. This is usually chosen so that there will be a reasonable number of data elements in each interval, and so that all of the data does not fall into a single interval or very few of them. This is somewhat a trial and error process. In this case, we have chosen a class interval of 5 years. The resulting intervals are 10-14 years, 15-19, 20-24, 25-29, 30-34, 35-39, 40-44, 45-49, 50-54, 55-59, 60-64, 65-71 years. You will notice that we extended the last interval just a bit to include the last piece of data (71 years old). It may appear that there are only four years in each interval (for example, 19 - 15 = 4), but there really are 5: (15, 16, 17, 18, 19).

Third, build the frequency distribution. This is done through the vehicle of a tabulation table as illustrated in Table V, page 74. For each piece of data, a hash mark is placed in the appropriate interval. When you're done, tally the hash marks and plot them on a graph, the "frequency distribution curve," as shown in figure 3. The example was for a church with 311 members. (Notice that we added up the frequencies in the far right column. This was just a check to see that we hadn't missed any of the data.)

Objectifying the Facts of Growth

Notice how "graphically" the frequency distribution curve illustrates the age distribution of the congregation. As you might expect, the majority were in the 20-39 range in ages.

When dealing with membership, it also is useful not only to plot the frequency distribution curve for the whole congregation, but to do this for men and women separately. When these are placed back-to-back, and drawn as a bar graph (rather than a continuous line), you get what looks like a Christmas tree. This is illustrated by Table VI and Figure 4, page 75.

USING COMPARATIVE DATA

The facts of growth can also be objectified by comparative techniques. Already attention has been directed to the necessity of comparing the growth rate of the group under study and other groups working with the same peoples. Such comparisons yield insights in analyzing growth or non-growth.

A second type of comparison that may pay dividends is comparing variables on questionnaires. For example, is there a difference in the attitudes of younger missionaries and older missionaries in regard to subsidy? Is there any correlation between members won in campaigns and those saved in regular services in regard to faithfulness and service? Other comparisons that can supply important insights will suggest themselves.

The most efficient way of finding correlations is through use of modern computer technology. However, this technique demands the help of trained personnel. It may well be beyond the reach of many, if not most, surveys.

Comparing growth with the projection of biological growth is another valuable comparison in objectifying church growth facts. Gerber points out that it has

TABLE V

Intervals	Tabulation	Frequency
65-70	`||`	2
60-64	`|||`	3
55-59	卌	5
50-54	卌 卌 `|`	11
45-49	卌 卌 卌 卌 `|`	21
40-44	卌 卌 卌 卌 卌 `|||`	28
35-39	卌 卌 卌 卌 卌 卌 `|`	31
30-34	卌 卌 卌 卌 卌 卌 卌 卌 卌 卌	55
25-29	卌 卌 卌 卌 卌 卌 卌 卌 卌 卌 卌 卌 卌 卌 卌 `|`	76
20-24	卌 卌 卌 卌 卌 卌 卌 卌 `||`	42
15-19	卌 卌 卌 卌 卌	25
10-14	卌 卌 `||`	12
	Total	311

FIGURE 3
Frequency Distribution Curve

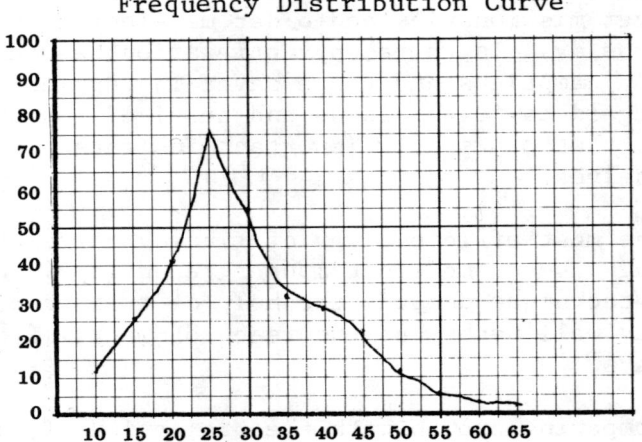

Objectifying the Facts of Growth 75

TABLE VI

Intervals	Tabulation		Frequency		
	Men	Women	Men	Women	Total
65-70		‖	0	2	2
60-64	/	//	1	2	3
55-59	//	///	2	3	5
50-54	⊞	⊞ /	5	6	11
45-49	⊞ ⊞	⊞ ⊞ /	10	11	21
40-44	⊞ ⊞ ⊞	⊞ ⊞ ///	15	13	28
35-39	⊞ ⊞ ⊞ /	⊞ ⊞ ⊞	16	15	31
30-34	⊞ ⊞ ⊞ ⊞ ⊞ ⊞	⊞ ⊞ ⊞ ⊞ ⊞	30	25	55
25-29	⊞ ⊞ ⊞ ⊞ ⊞ ⊞ ⊞	⊞ ⊞ ⊞ ⊞ ⊞ ⊞ ⊞ /	35	41	76
20-24	⊞ ⊞ ⊞ ⊞	⊞ ⊞ ⊞ ⊞ //	20	22	42
15-19	⊞ ⊞ /	⊞ ⊞ ////	11	14	25
10-14	⊞	⊞ //	5	7	12
		Totals	150	161	311

FIGURE 4

Frequency Distribution: Bar Graph of Men and Women

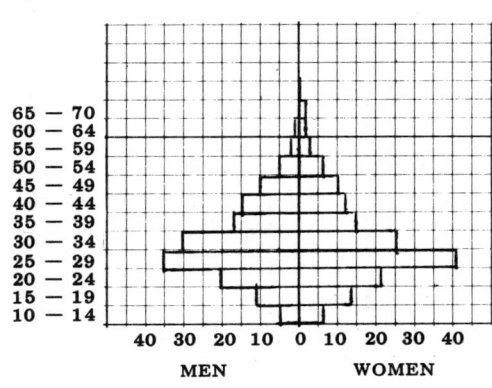

been estimated that a church would usually grow by
25% per decade by biological growth alone. This is
an average annual growth rate of about 2% per year.
Thus, if a church's growth is only 2% per year, it
is growing only by winning the children of members
(1973:50-51). Winning the children of members is
important. However, churches do not grow by biological growth alone. Therefore, the growth of the
church must be compared with the projection of biological growth.

The comparison of conversion/transfer growth and
biological growth can be objectified by a graph.
Plot on semi-logarithmic graph paper a solid line
showing the average growth for the past ten years.
Then plot the projected biological growth for the
same period. (Note, a projection is a straight line
only on semi-log paper.) One might realize a graph
as seen below on this page in Figure 5. This graph
represents the average growth of the Presbyterian
Church of Brazil with a solid line and the projected
biological growth with a broken line (based on statistics from Read, Monterroso, Johnson, 1969:71).

FIGURE 5

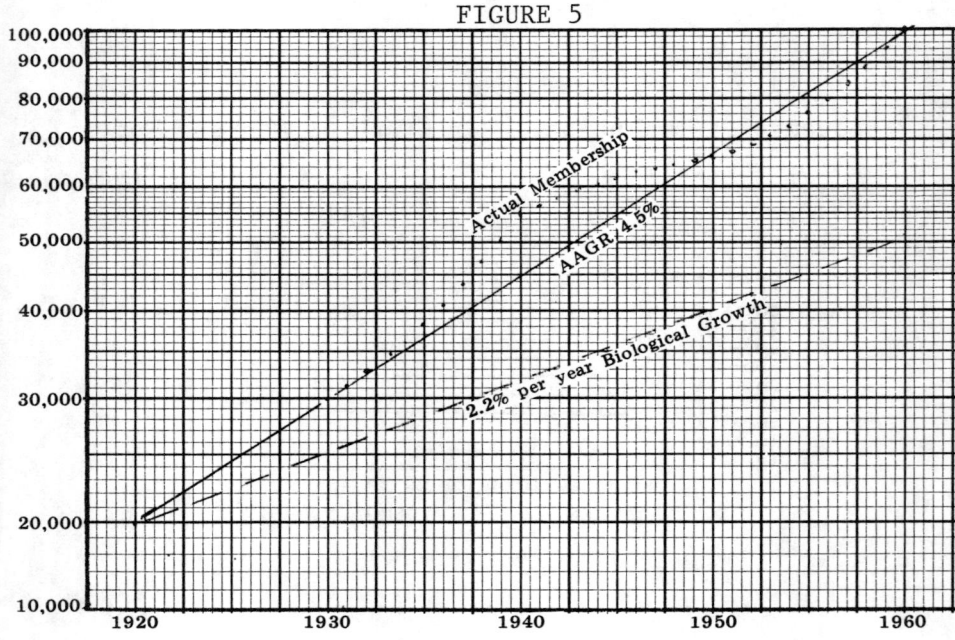

Objectifying the Facts of Growth

Obviously, the overall growth of the church exceeded the 2% per year projected for biological growth. However, during the decade 1940-1950, the church's growth lagged behind this figure. Recall from the section on drawing graphs or rates of growth that growth rate is proportional to the steepness of the curve. In this period, the fact that the actual membership curve (represented by the dotted line) was not as steep as the one for biological growth indicates that growth of the church fell behind biological growth. Comparisons such as this reveal much about church growth and also raise questions that are important for further study. Note well that all such comparisons can be made merely by plotting, without doing any calculations at all.

Comparing actual growth and projected biological growth helps a group realize the necessity of accelerating evangelism in the world. No one minimizes the winning of family members from Christian homes. However, McGavran is talking about the best and truest kind of growth when he says, "Nothing produces growth except baptisms from the world, provided those being baptized are properly shepherded and become vital Christians" (1970:90).

CONCLUSION

The facts of growth, though faithfully and painstakingly gathered, may still not tell the whole story. They need to be coaxed and prodded through the tools of graphs, frequency distribution curves, growth rates, and so on. They need to be objectified. Only then do they expose themselves to analysis. Only then can their implications be grasped and their full impact felt and understood. Be sure you do your plotting first, *before* you arrive at your conclusions. Objectifying is more important to analysis than it is in selling your conclusions to others, although the latter is a valuable side benefit where you have done your work well.

In the next Chapter we will continue this line of thinking and see how to analyze and interpret the facts we now have before us.

6
Digesting the Facts of Growth

Survey effort, up to this point, actually constitutes the all-important preliminary to the analyzing and interpreting phase. The facts, carefully gathered and clearly objectified, must be analyzed as to their meaning and evaluated with regard to planning and goal setting. Digesting the facts of growth occupies a central place in a Church Growth Survey.

ANALYZING THE FACTS OF GROWTH

To know when and in what areas a Church has grown is instructive. To understand attitudes and facts about churches, members, leaders, missionaries and historical conditions is important. However, the all-pervading questions is, "Why?" The first step in digesting the facts of growth is analyzing the meaning of these facts.

In the interpreting process, the survey uses the graphs and comparative data which together constitute some of the most useful tools for analyzing and interpreting church growth. McGavran declares, "All thinking about the Church should be done against the graphs of growth, because when done without exact knowledge of how the Church has and has not grown, it is likely to find itself in error" (1970:109).

Using the graphs of the Church, the areas or homogeneous units, and the local congregations, the surveyors seek explanations for each rise, period of stagnation, and decline. The facts of growth will be analyzed to find the "why." Invalid reasons will be set aside. Care must be taken to guard against simplistic reasoning. Church growth, or non-growth, is seldom caused by single factors. Usually a syndrome of factors combines to cause growth or prevent it. These clusters of reasons must be sought. The task of analysis is demanding; it is the all-important step if church growth is to be understood.

The analytical process is illustrated by McGavran in his presentation of the growth of the Presbyterian Church in Taiwan between 1865 and 1900. The graph of growth for this Church reveals advance, decline, and a lengthy plateau.

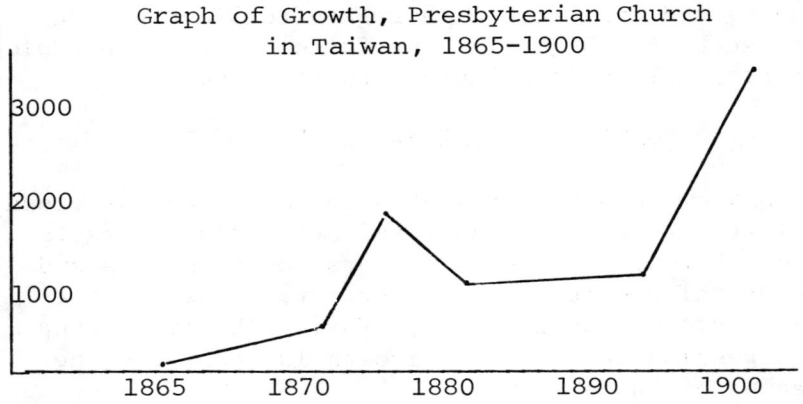

Graph of Growth, Presbyterian Church in Taiwan, 1865-1900

According to McGavran, this graph reveals five distinct periods of growth. The first, lasting about eight years, was the exploratory period of learning the Chinese language, local customs, buying land, and winning the first few Chinese converts. Around 1870 some 1500 Pepohwans, the aboriginal inhabitants of Taiwan, were brought into the Church. These Pepohwan Christians were shepherded, not in their language,

Digesting the Facts of Growth 81

but in Chinese. Consequently, many failed their baptismal examinations, and hence, were never baptized. The mission decided to concentrate on Chinese people and neglected the Pepohwans. These events largely explain the decline in the years before and after 1880. During the fourth period of growth, a long plateau denotes little advance. The Pepohwan movement had been arrested and few Chinese were becoming Christians.

Shortly after 1890, the graph reveals a surge upward. This surge followed the Japanese conquest of Taiwan in 1895. Chinese culture was discredited and under the impact of defeat when many Chinese became responsive to the Gospel. In addition, a remarkable missionary toured Taiwan. His preaching led to the conversion of many Chinese and the establishment of many small congregations.

The graph itself does not explain why the Church grew, declined, and plateaued. The causes of the growth, decline, and stagnation must be sought from historical materials and the memory of workers. The graph indicates when changes in the growth pattern took place and how long each period of growth lasted. It thus serves to "...break the meaningless whole into its meaningful parts, enabling the student of church growth to search for causes at the right times" (McGavran 1970: 111-113).

Another instructive graph is that of the Protestant Church on Nias, an island off the northwest coast of Sumatra. The Nias graph shows very slow growth from the beginning of Christianity in 1871 until 1915. The sudden surge of growth in 1915 slowed to a plateau between 1920 and 1925. After 1925 the graph reveals continued growth until the present.

Several factors explain the growth of the Nias Church. The slow beginning can be attributed to the state of the island before the Dutch established control. The missionaries were unable to serve outside the coastal cities. Many Nisans were headhunters. After the Dutch established law and built roads, the mission work proceeded until in 1915, when some 5,000 members were counted. In 1915 a great revival, known as "the great repentance," broke out. Under the influence of this revival, the membership of the Church leaped to 62,000 by 1921. (This was an average annual growth rate of 52%.) However, in 1925 the Church reported only 65,000 members. Such a plateau would ordinarily be attributed to a decline in growth rate. The records revealed no tendency toward consolidation. Consolidation, which is the neglecting of outreach *so that* existing works can be strengthened, often results in such slowing of growth.

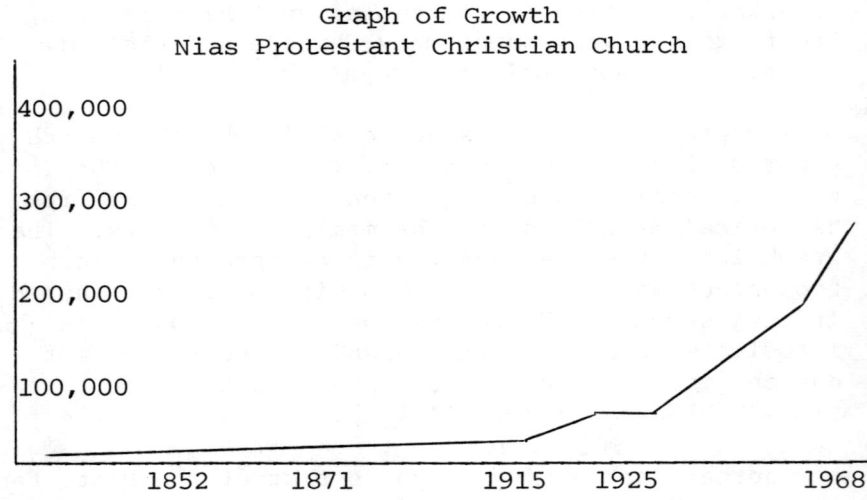

Graph of Growth
Nias Protestant Christian Church

Neither did records reveal any doctrinal, relational, or other problems. There seemed to be no explanation of this striking plateau in the growth of the Nias Church. However, secular history recorded an extended epidemic of flu that hit the island around 1919 and raged until 1923. Thousands died in the epidemic. This is the most likely explanation of the plateau. Although growth continued, death was removing unusually large numbers from the membership.

Digesting the Facts of Growth

After 1925, the epidemic eased and membership increase resumed. The Church was growing during the entire period of the epidemic but membership figures remained static due to unusually heavy death rates (cf. Smith 1970:94-96). Even so, from 1925 to 1968, the growth from 65,000 to 260,000 represents an average annual growth rate of only 3.3%.

Another instructive graph of growth is that of the Moluccan Protestant Church, also in Indonesia. This

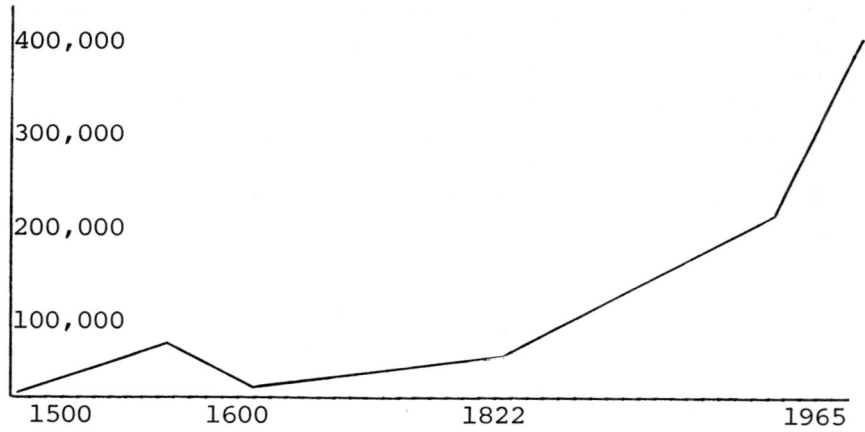

Graph of Growth
Moluccan Protestant Christian Church

graph reveals a Church that began in the 1530's, making it the oldest Protestant Church in Asia. By the 1590's, the Church numbered some 47,000 members. However, at the time the Dutch took over from the Portuguese in 1605, changing the Portuguese Catholic Churches to Dutch Protestant Churches, the membership had declined to around 13,000 members. Several factors combined to bring about this decline. In addition to improper shepherding, the wars led by Sultan Baab from Ternate, decimated many Christian villages. Thousands were martyred.

The Church continued to show meager growth until the period around 1775. Statistics are not presently available to make an accurate graph, but the real growth probably did not begin until the period around 1811 when the British Baptists, in the person of Jabez Carey, the third son of William Carey, ministered in the Moluccas (Ambon). Before Carey was forced to leave Ambon, Joseph Kam, another fine missionary, took up the task. Coupled with the effective church planting of these two missionaries was the formation of a mission group among the Ambonese that did much to spread the Gospel in these widespread islands. Even so, by calculating average annual growth rates in the two latter periods, we find historical events often combine with spiritual realities to cause growth. The following graph of the growth of Baptist Churches in two Indonesian cities (Semarang and Kediri) indicate spurts of growth around 1961 with a slowing between 1963-1965, followed by a period of explosive growth.

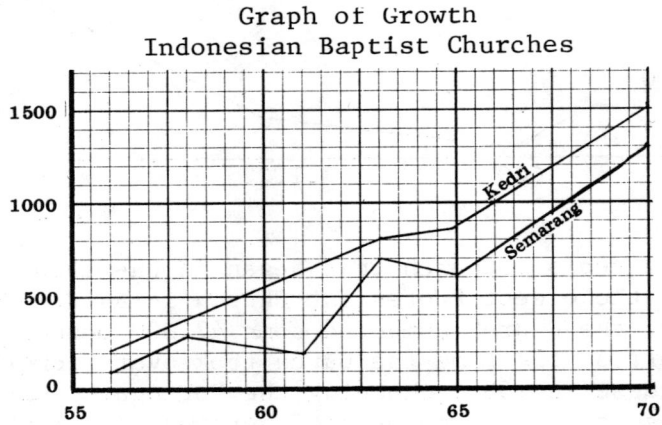

Graph of Growth
Indonesian Baptist Churches

Multiple factors must be considered in seeking reasons for this growth. In both cities, new evangelistic programs that emphasized planting churches began around 1961. The declining growth rate between 1963-1965 can be partially explained by the slowing of these two programs due to the departure of leadership. Even more serious was the build up of communist pressure, leading to the attempted coup of September 1965. During the period of 1963-1965, most Churches in Indonesia reported a marked decline in growth.

The explosive growth following 1965 can be attributed to the increased responsiveness in many regions of Indonesia after the communist failure. At the same time, a fruitful evangelistic campaign, emphasizing both personal evangelism and church planting, was promoted by the Baptist Churches in 1966-1967. This analysis of the growth of Baptist Churches in two areas seeks beneath the surface for causes of growth and non-growth (cf. Smith 1970:170-179).

Analysis must consider every aspect of growth. Virgil Gerber points out that if the growth pattern of a church consists of rises and declines, one might conclude that the church was not growing healthily. However, if analysis indicates that periodically members go out of this church to start new congregations, the conclusion would be reversed and the growth labeled robust. In such case, Gerber suggests a "family growth" graph, depicting the growth of the mother church and all its branches (1973:50-51).

A Church Growth Survey does not seek causes of growth in order to praise. Neither does it seek causes for non-growth in order to blame. The reason for seeking causes in both cases is that further growth might be stimulated. The analysis of church growth facts seeks to expose the reasons why churches grow stagnant, or decline so that roadblocks to growth can be avoided and greater results realized. McGavran says, "You recount what has happened in the past in order that you may judge what should happen in the future" (n.d.: p. 9).

The analysis must think courageously. There must be no simple defense of what has been done. Again, McGavran says,

If the Church has grown one hundred percent a decade, promotional thinking says, "How wonderful." Diagnostic thinking says, "With a ripe population, we should not limit ourselves to a mere one hundred per cent. How can we lift our expectation to God's level as we press forward with His command to disciple the nations?"

Analysis of the facts of growth should be shared with the entire membership of the organization being studied. A report should be prepared which analyzes and explains the facts gathered through the statistical studies, the drawing of graphs, the calculating of growth rates, the use of indigeneity scales, and the comparative data. This report should be distributed at least one month before the final phase of the survey begins.

This analytical report should show the meanings of the facts but not necessarily suggest new goals or plans. The final decision making and goal setting should involve the entire group and be based on the work of the evaluators (to be discussed in the following section). The analytical report is, then, a preliminary source of information. It will include graphs, insights gleaned from the questionnaires, and perhaps hints at needed changes. Every person involved in the group being studied should carefully consider the analysis report.

The analyzing phase of the survey lays the ground work for the next step, that of interpretation and recommendation.

INTERPRETING AND RECOMMENDING

The facts gathered and analyzed must be tested, evaluated, and interpreted before recommendations are prepared. To accomplish this task, it is highly advisable to seek help from outside the group under study. Insiders, no matter how knowledgeable and dedicated, seldom achieve the objectivity nor command the acceptance necessary. At this point in the survey, closeness to the situation has its disadvantages. The survey needs the stimulus of evaluators from outside to lead in its final stages.

Thus, a survey carried out by an individual or a small group will differ considerably. The remainder of the manual speaks of a group project. The individual or small group will serve as the evaluators and will compile a report and recommendations, much like the evaluators' report described. Hopefully, these recommendations will be heeded by the group involved. Therefore, an individual or small group making a survey should adapt the following suggestions to their particular needs.

The purpose of the evaluation and recommendation phase is not that of pointing a critical finger, but of finding more productive ways. The evaluators' report may indicate failings and weaknesses in previous patterns. The main purpose of the evaluation, however, is finding ways to increase church growth.

Evaluators should be selected with care. The importance of the evaluators can hardly be overstated. Their selection should be, therefore, a matter of deep concern, serious thought, and faithful prayer.

Evaluators should be objective, fair, and knowledgeable of church growth. They should be effective communicators. They should have experience in evangelistic ministry so as to have a practical viewpoint. At least one of the evaluators should have first hand understanding of the way the particular group functions. An evaluating team without definite understanding of the policies, ways of working, and relationships of the group is at a distinct disadvantage. While facility in the languages of the country is a decided advantage, it is not mandatory.

Evaluators must have vision and courage. They should be totally dedicated to world evangelization. They must be in physical condition that can stand the strain of weeks of intensive work. They must be willing to take a stand and be criticized for it. They must be emotionally stable enough to absorb the many failures, bad attitudes, and personal tragedies they will encounter. They must command the respect of the group. Such men are not easily found; they are available.

The inclusion of non-western evaluators greatly strengthens a survey effort. Many capable and dedicated men from non-western countries could make a significant contribution to any survey. It is highly recommended that non-western evaluators be included in the survey.

So important are the evaluators to the survey that it is advisable to give the group some voice in their selection. The steering committee might prepare a list of possible evaluators and allow the group a choice among them. Such a procedure could likely incorporate more people into the spirit of the survey.

Evaluators should be chosen at least one year (ideally longer) before the final period of the survey work. Those who can serve effectively are busy people with great demands on their time. To secure their services, early request is imperative. The committee should seek evaluators among missionaries, pastors, denominational leaders, professors of evangelism and missions, and other qualified persons.

An additional factor in securing evaluators early is the possibility that one or more of them might work with the steering committee in the preparation phases of the survey. Moreover, the early selection of evaluators provides them more opportunity to prepare for their service. Early decision on personnel pays dividends.

Digesting the Facts of Growth

The preliminary work of the evaluators consists of mastering the total body of facts discovered by the survey. As information is uncovered it should be sent to the evaluators. They should receive copies of all correspondence, all background material, all articles and reviews, as well as the analysis report. The evaluators should be conversant with the history, social and anthropological background of the area, as well as the history of the Church or mission.

Evaluators should not consider their preparation complete without some study and review of interviewing techniques. They should avail themselves of some of the many sources of instruction on methods of conducting interviews. Good interview techniques will strengthen the evaluators' usefulness in the survey.

Preparing to serve as an evaluator in a Church Growth Survey is, therefore, no small task. One professor of missions assigned his classes a paper on the work of the group to be studied. The students and professor used the background study information for the survey. Each student prepared what he felt would be an adequate plan for evangelism to be used by the group. The professor personally graded each paper. The understanding of the situation thus gained was of inestimable value to his service in the survey.

The evaluators should visit as many places and interview as many people as possible during the time of the study. Through their study of the preliminary reports, the evaluators will have developed hypotheses concerning the work and its needs. They will have heard with care the facts presented in the preliminary reports. The period of interviewing gives opportunity to test their hypotheses and also the analysis produced by the committee. They will also seek new insights as to why the churches have or have not grown.

The evaluators will interview church leaders, pastors, members, and missionaries. Interviews with persons from other Churches to get their reactions to and suggestions for the group under study are helpful. During the interviewing process, the evaluators will work to uncover feelings and attitudes of nationals and missionaries that relate to church growth. They will be alert to opportunities to minister. They might be used to help cure tensions between workers, such as between nationals and missionaries, between missionaries and other missionaries, or between nationals and other nationals.

Special care must be taken in the investigation of institutions related to the group under study. Institutions sometimes are defensive of their status and feel threatened by surveys. The evaluators must convey the idea of fairness and of "no ax to grind." However, the survey must be totally honest in evaluating the service of every phase of the work, including institutions. It should suggest ways for increasing the effectiveness of the institutions.

For best results a member of the steering committee should accompany the evaluators to each region. The committee member will not participate in the interviews. He will, however, be available for consultation and to insure that the evaluators arrive at the right places.

The evaluation team should be together as much as possible. While they will often conduct interviews separately in order to cover more ground, they should have adequate opportunity to discuss their findings and consider possible recommendations. They must have time for prayer and fellowship.

Evaluators should be careful not to talk about the recommendations they plan to make. They will take care not to talk about one member of the group to other members. They will, however, remain willing

Digesting the Facts of Growth

listeners to whatever is said. Speaking critically of one segment of the group to another must be studiously avoided.

The evaluators have a unique educational opportunity. They will be talking with pastors and other leaders, many of whom will have but limited understanding of church growth. Some with whom they talk may have a defective vision of world evangelism. This opportunity to share the fruits of church growth insight and the vision of God's harvest must be fully utilized.

Evaluators also have an unexcelled spiritual opportunity. Because they are from the "outside," members of the group will share with them as they will not with members of their own group. Evaluators can, therefore, minister in unique ways. They should spend much time in prayer with the persons they interview. The many opportunities to share spiritual experiences should be seized.

Another opportunity of the evaluators is that of serving as corrective agents. Almost certainly, as the evaluators talk and observe, they will recognize shortcomings, failings, and special needs of some members of the group. The evaluators can be of great service in pointing out needed personal improvements to some members of the group if they employ tact and speak in love.

Through interviewing and first-hand observation, the evaluators will come to mature insights into the needs of the situation. These insights should lead to definite recommendations. A written report of these recommendations forms the foundation for the decision-making phase of the survey.

The evaluators should present a written report at the decision meeting. At least one week, ideally ten days, should be reserved for preparing the evaluator's final report and recommendations. During this time

the evaluators should have constant access to some
members of the steering committee. The need for
further questions and consultations and to "try out"
some of the insights and recommendations often arises.

In writing their report, the evaluators must remember the importance of wording or connotation.
They should avoid words and phrases that unnecessarily arouse negative feelings. In one survey, the
evaluators found negative reactions to the term
"house church." The problem was alleviated by using
the term, "churches that meet in houses." Evaluators
must be sensitive to discover such feelings and avoid
needlessly arousing resistance.

The evaluators' report will be based on and interpret all the survey materials. Important facts will
be emphasized. Points at which the survey analysis
is either substantiated or contradicted will be mentioned. New insights discovered by the evaluators
will be shared. All that has gone before will be
funneled into this final report.

The report will fairly, clearly, and courageously
indicate both strengths and weaknesses in the work.
Since the purpose of the survey is improvement, there
may be more emphasis on weaknesses than on strengths.
When one goes to the doctor for a backache, he does
not expect an optimistic report on his lungs. Still,
the report should be both positive and negative. One
evaluation report began with a section entitled "The
Evaluation of a Good Foundation."

The report of the evaluators should contain definite recommendations. These recommendations should
be prayerfully reached and seriously presented.
Reasons for each recommendation should be given.
Included in the recommendations should be suggestions
for goals, changes in methods, and new directions
that would in the minds of the evaluators increase
the harvest. The recommendations will likely include

ideas for entirely new ways of working and suggestions for increasing the effectiveness of existing programs.

Goals should be a part of the evaluators' report. Gerber suggests that goals should be based on research, set in the spirit of prayer, and projected by faith. Goals should also, according to Gerber, be realistic and take full account of the projected biological growth that can be expected (1973:58-59).

There has been resistance to the idea of setting goals. This feeling that goal-setting is unspiritual is unfounded. There is nothing unspiritual about planning definitely for the salvation of men and the more effective growth of churches. Goal-setting is basically planning for advance.

Goals are useful in directing the ministry of any group. While they are never substitutes for the power of the Holy Spirit, goals determine direction; without goals, any direction is acceptable. Goals also determine the quality of the performance; no goals means any level of performance is acceptable. Without goals, it becomes easy to lower immediate objectives when obstacles are encountered. Goals reveal drifting and neglect. Goals stimulate to maximum effectiveness. Goals are useful tools for getting the job done and are not propaganda for spectators. They are pointers showing the way to objectives.

Planning, including goals, is at least as important to evangelistic endeavors as to the business world where planning is an established technique. McGavran quotes an article from *Fortune* magazine in which Gilbert Burck declares, "Knowledge is power and control, provided it is timely, ample, and relevant. Only a businessman who knows what is happening inside his company as soon as it happens can truly adjust his means to his aims" (McGavran 1967:197).

In response to this article, McGavran reveals his belief in planning and goals for mission work, saying:

Mission planning, of the magnitude of business planning already being done by bold corporations reported above, *could be done.* Would it be pleasing to God? The answer must be a resounding *yes.* God wants His lost children found. God wants all men to know the way of salvation provided in Jesus Christ according to the Scriptures. If nineteenth century planning already being done by many denominations and missionary societies on a small scale is pleasing to God, twentieth century planning on a large scale using all the planning devices now available will be even more pleasing. (Ibid.)

Obviously, goals and planning have an important function in effective evangelism. The evaluators should, therefore, incorporate goals in their recommendations. The goals may come as much from the ideas of members, heard in interviews, as from the evaluators themselves. From whatever source, the goals should suggest definite directions and should be considered by the entire group.

To those who still doubt the value of goals, the writer of Proverbs replies, "Any enterprise is built by wise planning, becomes strong through common sense, and profits wonderfully by keeping abreast of the facts" (Proverbs 24:3-4 Living Bible).

Evaluators' recommendations should be both visionary and attainable. These recommendations should not, however, be exclusively the work of the evaluators. They will have been gathered through the interviews and in consultation with the steering committee. The recommendations then, form the heart of all the work that has gone into the Church Growth Survey.

After the final recommendations have been written, but before they are reproduced, it is well to have an opportunity for the evaluators to meet with the entire steering committee. The proposed report will be shared, discussed, and perhaps altered on the basis of valid suggestions. The steering committee will guard against "leaking" the contents of the recommendations before the time of presentation.

The survey now has progressed to the point of projecting definite recommendations for action. Action must be taken by the body. The stage is thus set for the decision-making, which is the subject of the following chapter.

7
Making Decisions Based on the Survey

Surveys are designed to find and interpret the facts of church growth. They provide a foundation for decisions that lead to more effective methods of evangelism. Thus, when the survey reaches the point of decision-making, it attains the purpose for which it was created.

These decisions include new goals, policies, and methods. Efforts of gathering, objectifying, analyzing, and interpreting the facts of growth look forward to this all-important step. To understand the facts of growth and to see ways of enlarging the harvest, and then, to fail to make the decisions that will result in this greater harvest, is to refuse to take the most vital and fruitful step.

This chapter projects one plan for carrying out the decision-making process. Other plans might better meet the situation in other groups. Each group will make decisions and lay plans in accord with their special needs and procedures.

CONSIDERING THE RECOMMENDATIONS

The decisions must rest squarely on the facts revealed by the survey. Therefore, before coming to the decision meeting, every member of the group

Decisions Based on Church Growth Survey

should carefully study all survey materials. A letter, sent about a month before the decision meeting, reminding the members of the need for this study and the church growth reading materials can stimulate preparation.

The evaluators' report, including their recommendations, should be heard at the same time by the entire group. Since a greater impact is achieved when the recommendations are received at the same time by the group, it is better to wait until after the presentation to distribute printed copies. Thus, with the exception of the steering committee, the entire group should hear the recommendations together.

The decision-making session should begin with the reading of the evaluators' report and recommendations. This is not the time for persuading or impressing but simply an opportunity to convey the recommendations. It should be made clear that the recommendations are just that. They will be subsequently discussed, adapted, altered, and finally adopted (or rejected) by the group.

DISCUSSING THE RECOMMENDATIONS

Having heard the evaluators' recommendations, the group will begin discussion. Time should be given for a careful reading of the report and recommendations after the public reading. Members should be encouraged to write questions and viewpoints for consideration in the discussions.

The group should select a person to preside during the discussions. Usually this moderator should be from outside the group itself. He should be, however, known and respected by the group. The moderator should have first-hand knowledge of the group. He should understand, and be in sympathy with, the purpose and intention of the survey. Neither the evaluators nor the regularly elected leader of the group should serve as the moderator of the discussions.

Before the discussion period actually begins, the steering committee should announce subcommittees to deal with various sections of the evaluators' report. These subcommittees should be selected at the final meeting of the steering committee and the evaluators. A member of the steering committee may well serve as chairman of each of these subcommittees.

Since subcommittees are required for each section of the evaluators' report and since the report for every survey will be different, a different set of subcommittees will be demanded for each survey. However, most surveys will need subcommittees for: evangelism; theological education (leadership training); other institutions (medical, publication, social); life style (missionary and/or national leaders); relations with other groups. The group will select a subcommittee for each of the types of work in which it engages.

These subcommittees compile the results of the discussion on the section assigned to them. During the discussions, the members of the subcommittees stay alert to suggestions for modifications or additions to the evaluators' recommendations. After the discussion period, each subcommittee prepares a final list of recommendations to be considered and adopted by the group.

After the public and private reading of the evaluators' recommendations and before the actual discussion begins, there should be a period of questions from the group to the evaluators. The purpose of this period is clarification. The evaluators will try to explain the statements made and the recommendations advanced. The evaluators should not be defensive. They should merely answer questions relating to the report.

After this period of clarification, the evaluators serve only as resource persons. They should participate but little in the discussions, usually only when directly called upon. They should, however, contribute relevant church growth information.

With these preliminaries concluded, the group begins the discussions. In order to insure that all parts of the report and recommendations are discussed, it is advisable to set a time limit on the discussion of each section. Members should consider their contributions and express them as concisely as possible. The moderator must keep discussion within the time limits.

A spirit of freedom should be sought to insure that all opinions are expressed. Members with doubts and problems relating to some recommendations should be heard and respected. There should be no feeling of being forced. Every effort to achieve a consensus should be expended.

Members will be encouraged to suggest additional recommendations. Freedom to project changes in recommended goals and plans must be maintained. Both members and evaluators should be encouraged to contribute related church growth data and experiences to the discussions.

The discussion should continue as long as profitable and within the time limits. At some points, the moderator may feel it advisable to hold a "straw vote" to help the related subcommittee ascertain the spirit and mind of the group. At the end of the discussion period on a section of the report--for example, evangelism--the subject is entrusted to the subcommittee.

After the discussion period, the subcommittees assume the important function of preparing the final recommendations for the group's consideration. They have access to all the materials prepared by the survey, to the evaluators' report, and to the suggestions from the discussions. The subcommittee for each section attempts to capture the mind and will of the group in relation to each recommendation in their area.

The recommendations of the subcommittee may be either similar to, or totally different from, those of the evaluators. The subcommittee may add some recommendations not in the evaluators' report; it may delete other recommendations; it may modify or alter other recommendations. Those recommendations felt to be valid and well-supported in the discussions may be projected by the subcommittee more or less as suggested by the evaluators.

After carefully and prayerfully considering all factors, each subcommittee prepares a written report of recommendations on their section. These recommendations are submitted to the entire group. With these final recommendations from the subcommittees, the foundation for decision-making is well established.

ADOPTING THE RECOMMENDATIONS

Care should be taken that the recommendations from each subcommittee are compatible with all others. For example, one group felt that they should concentrate evangelistic efforts in the villages. This new plan of evangelism involved planting thousands of small groups that would meet in homes and other facilities. The group realized that to carry out this plan they would have to provide training for the thousands of leaders who would serve these small groups. Obviously, one central training school could not provide this training. Therefore, theological training was expanded to include training by extension so as to provide for the leaders envisioned. The evangelistic goals and the plans for training were seen to be mutually dependent and were therefore compatible.

Because many segments of the work will be mutually dependent, it is advisable to hear all the reports of the subcommittees before beginning the final discussions. In this way, recommendations can be brought in line one with another. As discussions proceed, some of the recommendations may be rejected and others modified. However, since previous discussion has considered all angles of the questions, most of the subcommittees' recommendations will likely be adopted.

The process of adoption will follow the group's usual procedures for decision-making. After the recommendations have been thoroughly considered, the group formally adopts those judged to be valid and compatible with God's will. The adopted recommendations become the group's goals, policies, and methods of work.

Ideally, the decisions will enjoy wide support. Inevitably, however, some will be unconvinced of the need for, or the wisdom of, some of the new goals, policies, and methods. Recommendations for changes and new methods invariably produce adverse reactions. The feelings and viewpoints of these persons should be understood and respected but not necessarily followed.

Final decisions, including goals, should be expressed in a series of compact, succinct statement of policy. Having been adopted by the entire group, these statements provide guidelines for the future work of the Church, mission, congregation, or other group. Every member should be provided with a personal copy of these policy statements.

CONCLUSION

When the decisions have been made and written into policy statements and the goals, policies, and methods have been set, the survey, in one sense, is over. The most important function, however, awaits fulfillment—implementing the decisions. The next chapter considers ways and means of implementation.

8
Implementing The Decisions

This manual has consistently emphasized the pragmatic nature of Church Growth Surveys. Uncovering information about and setting forth causes for church growth (or lack of growth), however important, are but preliminary goals of Church Growth Surveys. The major purpose is to reach the goals and implement the decisions so as to attain more effective evangelism. This final section deals with methods of reaching the goals and implementing the plans growing out of the decisions of the survey.

COMMUNICATING THE DECISIONS

An important step in implementing the decisions is a careful and accurate communication of these decisions to all affected. No group lives to itself; others invariably are affected by any group's decisions. Effective communication, resulting in fuller understanding and the greater likelihood of support, contributes significantly to the implementation of the decisions and goals.

The decisions reached through the survey must be communicated to fellow workers. As mentioned earlier, when a Church projects a survey, the mission with which the Church cooperates will be affected. When

Implementing the Decisions

a mission projects a survey, the Church related to that mission will be likewise affected. Therefore, the group that projects a survey is obligated to communicate the content of and reasons for the decisions.

Respect and consideration for fellow workers, who will be affected, demands that the decisions be explained. To present a statement of the decisions, goals, and projected new methods--without explanations--may create resistance rather than cooperation in realizing the goals. When surveys are not joint projects, careful, understanding and respectful communication is imperative.

A mission that projected a survey benefited by holding mission-financed seminars in the different geographical areas at which the decisions, new policies, and goals were explained and discussed. Through these seminars, the Church that worked with this mission heard first-hand the decisions that had been reached and the goals that had been set. Questions were answered as to the reasons behind the decisions and changes. The understanding gained formed a foundation for effective cooperation in implementing the decisions.

The task of communicating the decisions to fellow workers is obviously most demanding when the survey is not a joint venture. However, when a Church holds a survey, it is impossible that all members of the congregations attend the decision-making meeting. In this case, the group making the decisions (convention, congress, church conference, etc.) must strive to communicate to every member and every congregation, the content and spirit of the decisions and goals and seek their support.

Understanding promotes cooperation; misunderstanding spawns distrust and resistance. Therefore no effort should be spared in communicating the decisions to fellow workers. The implementation of the decisions will be significantly furthered by the response of those who will join in the effort to accomplish the goals. Proper communication increases the likelihood of positive response and active cooperation.

The decisions reached through the survey must be communicated to the home base. Many surveys involve groups such as missions that have ties with boards, societies, or Churches located outside the country in which the survey is conducted. In such cases, this support base should be given a considerate, careful, and complete explanation of the decisions and the reasons therefore. Respect for those who support the work demands no less.

In communicating with the home base, care should be taken to explain fully enough to insure that misunderstandings do not occur. The decisions and the new patterns should be examined for phrases that might create problems and misunderstandings in the minds of supporters. The explanations should be designed to avoid such problems.

A mission will have missionaries on furlough when the decisions and goals related to the survey are reached. These members should have been kept informed of the progress of the survey. They should have received all the materials. Special efforts should be made to communicate the decisions and new plans to those members who are not present at the decision-making meeting. Members of the group who do not attend meetings where decisions are reached often experience difficulties in understanding and accepting them. In this case again, understanding promises a greater degree of cooperation.

The results of the survey, including the decisions and goals, will usually be communicated also to interested parties not organizationally related to the group surveyed. Such communication is both proper and beneficial. However, care should be taken that those who receive the reports should understand what parts should and should not be made public.

Implementing the Decisions 105

Full and considerate communication of the decisions and goals reached will further the implementation of the goals. Since implementation is the ultimate reason for the survey, the matter of communication assumes added significance. Communication of the decisions is, therefore, an imperative and important step.

REACHING THE GOALS

Reaching the goals constitutes the single most important phase of the survey. Failure to attain the goals and to implement the decisions means that the survey has failed in its ultimate objectives. This is not to say that the survey has been a total failure. The spiritual victories achieved, the insights acquired, the facts uncovered, and the unity gained, are all values in themselves. It remains, however, that the ultimate objective is missed. Until the survey results in increased church growth, it has not attained the preeminent reason for its existence.

There should be detailed plans for reaching every decision and goal related to the survey. These written plans for reaching each goal (referred to in Chapter 7) should include target dates for reaching each step toward these goals. These step-by-step plans serve as guidelines. Plans also constitute checklists to how the group is progressing toward the goals.

One mission projected an end to subsidy as a result of a survey. The plan for ending subsidy was set up on a step-by-step basis with a regular reduction over a period of several years. By the date projected, the subsidy was ended.

A Church projected a plan for leadership training involving centers in different areas on a definite schedule. The plan involved also a goal for attracting a specified number of leaders into the training program each year. Using the guidelines as checks, the group was able to chart its progress. Another group planned the assignment of evangelists to various regions in specific years. Such step-by-step planning, with target dates for each step, increases effectiveness and the implementation of goals.

Often, planning is not completed at the initial decision-making meeting. Subsequent consultation and consideration provide further opportunities for planning. At these subsequent meetings, plans are often modified. By whatever method they are formed and realized, definite plans for reaching each goal must be formed and expressed in written guidelines. Such planning enhances implementation.

There should be full use of long-range planning in reaching the decisions related to the survey. One method of long-range planning, PERT planning (Performance Evaluation Review Technique), provides aids for reaching goals. It consists basically of planning backwards. The planners look first at the goals. Then, they plan backward to the present, considering steps that must be reached (and in what order) to insure the final goal. PERT planning considers the various facets of need in attaining each goal.

As a result of a survey, one group felt impressed to adopt a goal of one million souls in ten years. Such a goal seemed unrealistic until PERT planning showed the feasibility of the goal. Planning charts indicated that in order to have one million members, there would have to be at least 41,316 churches of various sizes. Leadership needs at these churches demanded a minimum of 23,336 leaders. Training this number of leaders demanded in addition to the central campus, at least 25 regional schools. Each of the regional schools, working on the extension plan, would need to project 20 teaching centers, making a total of 500 teaching centers. With 50 students in each center (over the ten years period) the total of trained leaders would reach 25,000 in a decade.

Implementing the Decisions

The projected growth was plotted on a chart, and intermediate goals were filled in. Such a chart is reproduced on page 108. PERT involves much more than this and deserves looking into.*

A second method of long-range planning that holds great promise for church growth research, consists of preparing a "program base design." A program base design is the stated pattern of work which is used for developing comprehensive and strategic long-range plans. The base design is developed from twelve elements: biblical foundations, historical backgrounds, philosophy, needs, basic intentions, program structure, program relationships, organization, human resources, physical resources, financial resources and administrative controls (guidance). A well-constructed base design not only helps the group in planning and reaching goals, but also explains the group's procedures to cooperating bodies.**

There should be earnest prayer and effort toward reaching the decisions growing out of the survey. The decisions relating to church growth are related to spiritual realities. The goals will be attained only through genuine effort and earnest prayer. Prayer and work remain the foremost elements in implementing the projected goals.

---

* Groups hoping to make use of PERT planning techniques should obtain the book, *Planning and PERT*, from the Missions Advanced Research and Communication Center, 919 W. Huntington Drive, Monrovia, Ca. This book is indispensible for PERT planning.
** The development of program base designs is thoroughly discussed in the guide, "East Asia Planning Manual," prepared for use by the Southern Baptist Mission in Taiwan, Okinawa, Japan, Korea, and Hong Kong-Macao.

10-YEAR PROJECTED GROWTH CHART

Top figure indicates the number of congregations and the bottom figure the total numbers in these congregations

SIZE OF church	1972	1973	1974	1975	1976	1977	1978	1979	1980	1981	1982
5-20	32 / 250	97 / 850	184 / 1800	330 / 3000	550 / 5500	910 / 9000	1540 / 15500	2750 / 28000	4800 / 48000	8350 / 84000	13800 / 137000
20-75	52 / 1600	62 / 2100	106 / 5000	184 / 9000	242 / 13200	400 / 20000	663 / 33500	1100 / 54000	1800 / 90000	3000 / 150000	4600 / 230000
75-150	13 / 1100	15 / 1600	20 / 1800	30 / 2700	41 / 4200	58 / 6000	90 / 9300	135 / 13000	200 / 21000	300 / 30000	460 / 45000
150-400	11 / 2400	12 / 2500	13 / 2600	14 / 2900	15 / 3600	18 / 4500	25 / 7600	38 / 11,000	61 / 19000	80 / 24000	120 / 35000
400-600	0 / 0	1 / 400	2 / 800	2 / 900	3 / 1100	3 / 1500	4 / 2100	6 / 3000	10 / 4000	14 / 7000	18 / 8000
600-1400	0 / 0	0 / 0	0 / 0	0 / 0	0 / 0	0 / 0	1 / 800	1 / 1000	2 / 2000	3 / 3000	5 / 5000
Total members	108 / 5350	187 / 7450	325 / 12000	560 / 18500	869 / 27600	1389 / 41000	2323 / 68,800	4033 / 115000	6873 / 184000	11,747 / 298000	19003 / 460000

Implementing the Decisions

Planning without producing is self-defeating. The survey provides a foundation for change that should lead to more effective church growth. Plans, however valid; decisions, however courageous; goals, however far-reaching; do not insure church growth. The ministry of the Holy Spirit, working through Christians, produces church growth.

There should be a willingness to modify plans as the need for modifications is realized. The group must feel that the goals and methods set forth in the recommendations are valid. They should have a sense of God's leadership in each decision reached. Yet, as the group moves into the stage of implementation, the need to modify some of the plans, goals, or other facets of the decisions will become apparent. When such need arises, the group should be willing to make such adjustments without turning from the basic thrust or spirit of the decisions. Additional research may indicate the need of further modification.

The purpose of church growth research is not to effect and defend a survey, nor the decisions thereof, but rather to find ways of attaining more effective church growth. Therefore, the group should be prepared to consider modifications in regard to the plans and goals adopted. Knowing when, and in what degree, to modify the decisions is often the most difficult phase of the entire survey.

There should be a committee to give guidance toward reaching each goal. This committee projects plans for attaining the particular goal or decision assigned to it. As the work progresses, the committee leads the group and keeps it informed of the progress or lack of progress toward that goal. Progress is more likely when a special committee is charged with definite responsibility for planning the implementation of each goal and decision.

Plans and goals must be implemented. Reaching the goals of the survey constitutes the ultimate test of the success of the venture. Implementation assumes major importance in concluding a survey.

PRESERVING THE RESULTS

The primary values of a Church Growth Survey lie in the plans that are conceived and the acceptance of goals, both of which increase evangelistic effectiveness. These values alone, however, do not exhaust the helpfulness of a Church Growth Survey. The information uncovered and insights gained have benefit independent of the implementation (or its failure).

Because of the value of church growth information in general, the entire body of material should be shared with interested parties outside the group studied. Departments of missions in colleges and seminaries, professors of missions, mission executives, church leaders, denominational offices of missions and evangelism, and many others profit greatly from all studies of church growth. The results of the survey should be shared as widely as resources allow (see Appendix C).

Materials prepared in the survey should also be preserved in a central place for future reference. Copies of the materials should be stored at the central office of the Church or mission. Other copies should be placed in the libraries of the schools related to the group studied.

Future value of the survey can be increased by compiling a complete record of the effort. To provide this record, a committee or an individual should be designated to write an historical account of the entire survey but with particular emphasis on the period of implementation.

This history will objectively describe the successes and failures in reaching the goals. It will evaluate objectives and methods of the survey and means by which goals are pursued.

Implementing the Decisions

Other surveys can avoid mistakes and incorporate strengths by studying the account of a survey. Every Church Growth Survey has value to all other students of church growth. The history of the survey thus has a value to all who are interested in why churches grow and multiply.

CONCLUSION

Implementing the decisions, therefore, occupies an important place in the survey effort. Decisions and goals attain little objective result until actually put into effect. Church growth information has independent value. Church Growth Surveys however, must not be content to simply provide this information, but rather must stimulate increased church growth. Thus, a Church Growth Survey must strive to see that goals are attained in order to reach its maximum effectiveness.

9
Conclusion

Church Growth Surveys involve extensive expenditures of time, effort, and material resources. Some might conclude that the mass of material demanded renders a survey so involved as to be impractical or impossible. Such is not the case.

Any group can conclude an effective survey by using the check list found in Appendix A of this manual. Situations will sometimes make finding some facts or achieving some steps impossible. Such deletions decrease the overall effectiveness of the survey but do not obviate its ultimate value. This manual describes an ideal survey and most will not attain full compliance with all suggestions. Effective surveys can be realized although some steps are impossible and some facts unavailable. Needless to say, the more fully these suggestions are followed, the more effective will be the survey.

The difficulties of carrying out a survey should not deter a group from the effort. He who sees only the difficulties may turn back. The writer of *Ecclesiastes* notes:

> He that observeth the wind shall not sow; and he that regardeth the clouds shall not reap (11:4).

Conclusion

Every group should proceed with a study of its growth. Church Growth Surveys are possible, practical, and imperative. They open new avenues for attaining the will of God in evangelism and church development. The Holy Spirit works with power through efforts at self-study. For these and many other reasons, every group should engage in a Church Growth Survey.

Appendixes

Appendix A
TABLE 1. AAGR

% growth increase	1	2	3	4	5	6	7	8	9	10	15	20	25	50	75
1%	1.00%	0.50%	0.33%	0.25%	0.20%	0.17%	0.14%	0.12%	0.11%	0.10%	0.07%	0.05%	0.04%	0.02%	0.01%
2%	2.00%	1.00%	0.66%	0.50%	0.40%	0.33%	0.28%	0.25%	0.22%	0.20%	0.13%	0.10%	0.08%	0.04%	0.03%
4%	4.00%	1.98%	1.32%	0.99%	0.79%	0.66%	0.56%	0.49%	0.44%	0.39%	0.26%	0.20%	0.16%	0.08%	0.05%
6%	6.00%	2.96%	1.96%	1.47%	1.17%	0.98%	0.84%	0.73%	0.65%	0.58%	0.39%	0.29%	0.23%	0.12%	0.08%
8%	8.00%	3.92%	2.60%	1.94%	1.55%	1.29%	1.11%	0.97%	0.86%	0.77%	0.51%	0.39%	0.31%	0.15%	0.10%
10%	10.00%	4.88%	3.23%	2.41%	1.92%	1.60%	1.37%	1.20%	1.07%	0.96%	0.64%	0.48%	0.38%	0.19%	0.13%
12%	12.00%	5.83%	3.85%	2.87%	2.29%	1.91%	1.63%	1.43%	1.27%	1.14%	0.76%	0.57%	0.45%	0.23%	0.15%
14%	14.00%	6.77%	4.46%	3.33%	2.65%	2.21%	1.89%	1.65%	1.47%	1.32%	0.88%	0.66%	0.53%	0.25%	0.17%
16%	16.00%	7.70%	5.07%	3.78%	3.01%	2.50%	2.14%	1.87%	1.66%	1.50%	0.99%	0.74%	0.56%	0.30%	0.20%
18%	18.00%	8.63%	5.67%	4.22%	3.37%	2.80%	2.39%	2.09%	1.85%	1.67%	1.11%	0.83%	0.65%	0.33%	0.22%
20%	20.00%	9.54%	6.27%	4.65%	3.71%	3.09%	2.64%	2.31%	2.05%	1.84%	1.22%	0.92%	0.73%	0.37%	0.24%
25%	25.00%	11.80%	7.72%	5.74%	4.56%	3.79%	3.24%	2.83%	2.51%	2.26%	1.50%	1.12%	0.90%	0.45%	0.30%
30%	30.00%	14.02%	9.14%	6.78%	5.39%	4.47%	3.82%	3.33%	2.96%	2.66%	1.76%	1.32%	1.05%	0.53%	0.35%
35%	35.00%	16.19%	10.52%	7.79%	6.19%	5.13%	4.39%	3.82%	3.39%	3.05%	2.02%	1.51%	1.21%	0.60%	0.40%
40%	40.00%	18.32%	11.87%	8.78%	6.96%	5.77%	4.92%	4.30%	3.81%	3.42%	2.27%	1.70%	1.35%	0.68%	0.45%
45%	45.00%	20.42%	13.19%	9.73%	7.71%	6.39%	5.45%	4.75%	4.21%	3.79%	2.51%	1.88%	1.50%	0.75%	0.50%
50%	50.00%	22.47%	14.47%	10.67%	8.45%	6.99%	5.96%	5.20%	4.61%	4.14%	2.74%	2.05%	1.64%	0.81%	0.54%
60%	60.00%	26.49%	16.96%	12.47%	9.85%	8.15%	6.94%	6.05%	5.36%	4.81%	3.18%	2.38%	1.90%	0.94%	0.63%
70%	70.00%	30.38%	19.35%	14.18%	11.18%	9.23%	7.85%	6.83%	6.05%	5.43%	3.58%	2.68%	2.13%	1.06%	0.70%
80%	80.00%	34.16%	21.64%	15.83%	12.47%	10.29%	8.76%	7.62%	6.75%	6.05%	3.98%	2.98%	2.38%	1.18%	0.79%
100%	100.00%	41.42%	25.99%	18.92%	14.87%	12.25%	10.41%	9.05%	8.01%	7.18%	4.73%	3.53%	2.81%	1.40%	0.93%
120%	120.00%	48.32%	30.06%	21.79%	17.03%	14.04%	11.92%	10.36%	9.16%	8.20%	5.40%	4.02%	3.20%	1.59%	1.05%
140%	140.00%	54.92%	33.91%	24.47%	19.03%	15.71%	13.32%	11.56%	10.22%	9.15%	6.01%	4.47%	3.56%	1.77%	1.17%
160%	160.00%	61.25%	37.51%	26.98%	21.06%	17.26%	14.63%	12.69%	11.20%	10.03%	6.58%	4.89%	3.90%	1.93%	1.28%
180%	180.00%	67.33%	40.95%	29.36%	22.85%	18.72%	15.85%	13.74%	12.12%	10.84%	7.11%	5.29%	4.20%	2.03%	1.38%
200%	200.00%	73.21%	44.22%	31.61%	24.57%	20.09%	16.99%	14.72%	12.98%	11.61%	7.60%	5.65%	4.50%	2.22%	1.43%
220%	220.00%	78.89%	47.36%	33.75%	26.19%	21.39%	18.08%	15.65%	13.80%	12.33%	8.06%	5.99%	4.75%	2.35%	1.55%
240%	240.00%	84.39%	50.39%	35.79%	27.73%	22.63%	19.12%	16.53%	14.57%	13.02%	8.50%	6.31%	5.02%	2.43%	1.60%
260%	260.00%	89.74%	53.26%	37.74%	29.23%	23.80%	20.09%	17.36%	15.30%	13.67%	8.91%	6.61%	5.26%	2.59%	1.72%
280%	280.00%	94.94%	56.05%	39.62%	30.66%	24.92%	21.01%	18.16%	15.99%	14.27%	9.31%	6.90%	5.49%	2.71%	1.80%
300%	300.00%	100.00%	58.74%	41.42%	31.95%	25.99%	21.91%	18.92%	16.65%	14.87%	9.68%	7.18%	5.72%	2.81%	1.87%
320%	320.00%	104.96%	61.34%	43.16%	33.24%	27.01%	22.75%	19.65%	17.29%	15.43%	10.04%	7.44%	5.91%	2.91%	1.93%
340%	340.00%	109.76%	63.86%	44.83%	34.51%	28.01%	23.57%	20.35%	17.90%	15.97%	10.38%	7.69%	6.11%	3.01%	1.99%
360%	360.00%	114.48%	66.31%	46.45%	35.69%	28.96%	24.36%	21.02%	18.48%	16.49%	10.71%	7.93%	6.29%	3.13%	2.06%
380%	380.00%	119.09%	68.69%	48.02%	36.85%	29.88%	25.12%	21.66%	19.04%	16.98%	11.02%	8.16%	6.48%	3.19%	2.11%
400%	400.00%	123.61%	71.00%	49.53%	37.97%	30.77%	25.85%	22.28%	19.58%	17.46%	11.33%	8.38%	6.65%	3.27%	2.17%
450%	450.00%	134.52%	76.52%	53.14%	40.63%	32.86%	27.58%	23.75%	20.85%	18.59%	12.04%	8.90%	7.06%	3.47%	2.30%
500%	500.00%	144.95%	81.71%	56.51%	43.10%	34.80%	29.17%	25.10%	22.03%	19.62%	12.69%	9.37%	7.43%	3.65%	2.42%
600%	600.00%	164.58%	91.29%	62.66%	47.58%	38.31%	32.05%	27.54%	24.14%	21.48%	13.85%	10.22%	8.09%	3.97%	2.63%
700%	700.00%	182.96%	100.00%	68.18%	51.57%	41.42%	34.59%	29.68%	25.99%	23.11%	14.87%	10.96%	8.67%	4.25%	2.81%
800%	800.00%	200.00%	108.01%	73.21%	55.19%	44.22%	36.87%	31.61%	27.65%	24.57%	15.78%	11.61%	9.19%	4.49%	2.97%
900%	900.00%	216.23%	115.44%	77.83%	58.49%	46.78%	38.95%	33.35%	29.15%	25.89%	16.59%	12.20%	9.65%	4.71%	3.12%
1000%	1000.00%	231.66%	122.39%	82.12%	61.54%	49.13%	40.85%	34.95%	30.53%	27.10%	17.33%	12.74%	10.07%	4.91%	3.25%
1500%	1500.00%	300.00%	151.98%	100.00%	74.11%	58.74%	48.60%	41.42%	36.05%	31.95%	20.30%	14.87%	11.73%	5.70%	3.77%
2000%	2000.00%	358.26%	175.89%	114.07%	83.84%	66.10%	54.40%	46.31%	40.25%	35.59%	22.50%	16.44%	12.95%	6.23%	4.14%
2500%	2500.00%	409.90%	196.25%	125.81%	91.88%	72.12%	59.17%	50.27%	43.62%	38.52%	24.26%	17.69%	13.95%	6.73%	4.46%
3000%	3000.00%	456.78%	214.14%	135.96%	98.73%	77.25%	63.22%	53.61%	46.46%	40.97%	25.73%	18.75%	14.72%	7.11%	4.69%
3500%	3500.00%	500.00%	230.19%	144.95%	104.77%	81.71%	66.85%	56.51%	48.91%	43.10%	26.99%	19.62%	15.41%	7.43%	4.89%
4000%	4000.00%	540.31%	244.80%	153.04%	110.15%	85.67%	69.98%	59.07%	51.08%	44.97%	28.09%	20.40%	16.01%	7.71%	5.08%
4500%	4500.00%	578.23%	258.30%	160.43%	115.06%	89.29%	72.80%	61.38%	53.02%	46.65%	29.08%	21.10%	16.55%	7.96%	5.24%
5000%	5000.00%	614.14%	270.81%	167.23%	119.52%	92.57%	75.36%	63.47%	54.79%	48.17%	29.97%	21.72%	17.03%	8.13%	5.38%
6000%	6000.00%	681.02%	293.65%	179.67%	127.56%	98.51%	79.91%	67.17%	57.90%	50.85%	31.53%	22.82%	17.87%	8.57%	5.63%
7000%	7000.00%	742.61%	314.10%	190.28%	134.56%	103.49%	83.85%	70.38%	60.58%	53.15%	32.87%	23.76%	18.59%	8.90%	5.85%
8000%	8000.00%	800.00%	332.67%	200.00%	140.82%	108.01%	87.54%	73.26%	62.95%	55.20%	34.04%	24.57%	19.22%	9.13%	5.98%
9000%	9000.00%	853.94%	349.79%	208.85%	146.50%	112.08%	90.49%	75.74%	65.07%	57.00%	35.08%	25.30%	19.77%	9.44%	5.20%
10000%	10000.00%	904.99%	365.70%	217.02%	151.63%	115.80%	93.34%	78.05%	66.99%	58.65%	36.03%	25.96%	20.27%	9.67%	5.35%

% growth increase →

TABLE 2.
Check List for Church Growth Surveys

How to use this check list: The check list is designed to direct the survey tasks in proper order. Each task and the pages in the *Manual* relating to it are listed in the first two columns. The next two columns give the ideal and the minimum time needed for each task. The deadlines relate to *the time before the end of the period of decision-making.* Tasks that continue throughout the period of the survey are indicated with a "C." Tasks that continue over a period of time are indicated by notations such as 1yr--3 mos, meaning the task begins one year before and ends three months before the decision meeting. The last three columns provide space to note when tasks are planned, begun, and finished. In this way, progress can be charted and tasks lagging behind can be given special attention.

TASKS	PAGES	DEADLINES		PROGRESS OF TASK		
		Ideal	Minimum	Planned	Begun	Finished
1. Investigating possibilities and seeking understanding	1-15	2,3yr	1 1/2yr			
2. Committing the group	16	2yr	1 1/2yr			
3. Securing Support	16-17	2yrC	1 1/2yrC			

TABLE II

4. Selecting Chairman	19-20	2 yr	1 1/2yr		
5. Selecting Steering Committee	17-20	1 1/2yr	10 mo		
6. Selecting Evaluators	87-89	1 1/2yr	6 mo		
7. Providing Background Material	20-24	1 1/2yr	6 mo		
8. Establishing a Church Growth base	24-25	1 yrC	6 moC		
1) Circulating printed materials	24	1yr-1mo	6mo-1mo		
2) Church Growth Seminars	24	9mo-1mo	6mo-1mo		
3) Translation of church growth materials	25	1yr-C	6mo-C		

TABLE II

			3mo. C			
4) Provision for continuing research	25					
9. Seeking the Facts of Growth		6mo. C	3mo. C			
1) Finding Statistics	26-54	1yr-1mo	6mo-1mo			
2) Questionnaires prepared, sampling planned	26-32	1yr-3mo	6mo-3mo			
3) Questionnaires tested	32-41	10 mo	4 mo			
4) Questionnaires used	32-41	9 mo	3 mo			
5) Questionnaires interpreted	32-41	7 mo	2 mo			
6) Tabulation of all data from statistics, questionnaires, etc.	32-41	6 mo	2 mo			
7) Determining indigeneity with scales	32-41	5 mo	1 mo			
	41-54	5 mo	1 mo			

TABLE II

10. Objectifying the Facts of Growth	55–78	6mo–3mo	3mo–1mo	
1) Calculating percentages and distributions	70–75	6mo–3mo	3mo–1mo	
2) Preparing graphs of growth	55–58	6mo–2mo	3mo–1mo	
3) Calculating growth rates	58–64	6mo–2mo	3mo–1mo	
4) Preparing graphs of growth rates	64–70			
5) Making valid comparisons	73–78	6mo–2mo	3mo–1mo	
11. Digesting the Facts of Growth	79–95	4mo–1wk	2mo–1wk	
1) Analyzing the Facts	79–86	4mo–1mo	2mo–1mo	
2) Study and Interviewing of the evaluators	86–95	2mo–2wk	1mo–1wk	
3) Preparing report of evaluators	91–95	2wk–1wk	1wk–1wk	

TABLE II

12. Making and Implementing Decisions	96-101	1wk-C	1wk-C
1) Considering recommendations	96-98	1wk	1wk
2) Selecting committee for each goal	109	2da-1da	1da-1da
3) Appointment of the historian	110-111	1da	1da
4) Communication with fellow workers	102-105	C	C
5) Communication with home base	104	C	C
6) Using PERT planning and other planning methods	105-109	C	C
7) Carrying out the decisions	109-111	C	C

Appendix B
Helpful Materials for Church Growth Surveys

A. *ARTICLES*

    KRAFT, Charles
        1963   "Christian Conversion or Cultural Conversion," *Practical Anthropology*, Vol. 10, No. 4: 179-86.
        1973   "Dynamic Equivalence Churches," *Missiology*, Vol. 1, No. 1:39-58.

    LARSON, Donald N.
        1963   "Church, Plaza, and Marketplace," *Practical Anthropology*, Vol. 10, No. 4: 167-74.

    LUZBETAK, Louis J.
        1963   "Toward An Applied Missionary Anthropology," *Practical Anthropology*, Vol. 10, No. 5: 199-208.

    McGAVRAN, Donald A.
        1964   "Nothing But the Truth," *Church Growth Bulletin*, Vol. 1, No. 1: 10.
        1964   "Is 'Little Growth' Cultural Overhang?" *Church Growth Bulletin*, Vol. 1, No. 2: 4, 5.
        1965   "Wrong Strategy: The Real Crisis in Missions," *International Review of Missions*, 54:451-61.
        1966   "Why Neglect Gospel-Ready Masses?" *Christianity Today*, Vol. 10:769-71.
        1967   "How Much Planning is Pleasing to God," *Church Growth Bulletin*, Vol. 10, No. 3: 196-97.
        1968   "Church Growth Strategy Continued," *International Review of Missions*, 57:335-43.

NOBLE, Lowell L.
   1962   "A Culturally Relevant Witness to Animists," *Practical Anthropology*, Vol. 9, No. 5:220-22.

REYBURN, William D.
   1960   "Identification in the Missionary Task," *Practical Anthropology*, Vol. 7, No. 1: 1-15.
   1970   "The Helping Relationship in Missionary Work," *Practical Anthropology*, Vol. 17, No. 2:49-59.

TABER, Charles R.
   1970   "The Missionary, Wrecker, Builder, or Catalyst?" *Practical Anthropology*, Vol. 17, No. 4:145-52.
   1970   "The Missionary Ghetto," *Practical Anthropology*, Vol. 18, No. 5:193-97.

SEAMANDS, John T.
   1967   "What McGavran's Church Growth Thesis Means," *Evangelical Missions Quarterly*, Vol. 3, No. 1:2-31.

TIPPETT, Alan R.
   1965   "Numbering: Right or Wrong?" *Church Growth Bulletin*, Vol. 1, No. 3:1-2.
   1966   "Church Growth or Else," *World Vision Magazine*, Vol. 12:28.
   1968   "Anthropology: Luxury or Necessity for Missions," *Evangelical Missions Quarterly*, Vol. 1:7-19.

WAGNER, C. Peter
   1973   "Evangelical Missions and Revolution Today," *Missiology*, Vol. 1, No. 1:91-98.

B. BOOKS

ALLEN, Roland
   1962   *Missionary Methods: St. Paul's or Ours?* Grand Rapids, Eerdmans.

APPENDIX B

ARN, Win and McGAVRAN, Donald A.
   1973   *How to Grow a Church.* Glendale, Calif. Regal Books.

BENNETT, Charles
   1968   *Tinder In Tabasco.* Grand Rapids, Eerdmans.

BRAUN, Neil
   1971   *Laity Mobilized.* Grand Rapids, Eerdmans.

COOLEY, Frank L.
   1968   *Indonesia: Church and Society.* New York, Friendship Press.

ENYART, Paul C.
   1970   *Friends in Central America.* South Pasadena, William Carey Library.

GERBER, Virgil
   1971   *Missions in Creative Tension.* South Pasadena, William Carey Library.
   1973   *A Manual for Evangelism/Church Growth.* South Pasadena, William Carey Library.

HODGES,
   1973   *A Guide to Church Planting.* Chicago, Moody Press.

McFALL, Ernest A.
   1970   *Approaching the Nuer of Africa Through the Old Testament.* South Pasadena, William Carey Library.

McGAVRAN, Donald A.
   1955   *The Bridges of God.* New York, The Friendship Press.
   1959   *How Churches Grow.* New York, The Friendship Press.
   1965   *Church Growth and Christian Mission.* New York, Harper and Row, Publishers.
   1970   *Understanding Church Growth.* Grand Rapids, Eerdmans.

McGAVRAN, Donald A. (Cont'd)
  1972 *The Eye of the Storm.* Chicago, Moody Press.
  1973 *Crucial Issues in Missions Tomorrow.* Chicago, Moody Press.
  n.d. *How to Do a Survey of Church Growth.* Pasadena, School of World Mission and Institute of Church Growth.
  1972 *Crucial Issues in Missions Tomorrow.*

MONTGOMERY, Jim
  1972 *New Testament Fire in the Philippines.* Manila, O.M.F. Press (D-GRIP).

OLSON, Gilbert W.
  1969 *Church Growth in Sierra Leone.* Grand Rapids, Eerdmans.

RANDALL, Max
  1970 *Profile for Victory: New Proposals for Missions in Zambia.* South Pasadena, William Carey Library.

READ, William R.
  1965 *New Patterns of Church Growth in Brazil.* Grand Rapids, Eerdmans.

READ, W. R., MONTERROSO, V. M., JOHNSON, H. A.
  1969 *Latin American Church Growth.* Grand Rapids, Eerdmans.

SHEARER, Roy E.
  1966 *Wildfire: Church Growth in Korea.* Grand Rapids, Eerdmans.

SMALLEY, William A.
  1967 *Readings in Missionary Anthropology.* South Pasadena, William Carey Library.

SMITH, Ebbie C.
  1970 *God's Miracles: Indonesian Church Growth.* South Pasadena, William Carey Library.

APPENDIX B

SUBBAMMA, B. V.
  1970 *New Patterns for Discipling Hindus.*
      South Pasadena, William Carey Library.

SWANSON, Alan J.
  1970 *Taiwan: Mainline Versus Independent Church Growth.* Pasadena, William Carey Library.

TIPPETT, Alan R.
  1967 *Solomon Islands Christianity.* South Pasadena, William Carey Library.
  1969 *Verdict Theology in Missionary Theory.*
      South Pasadena, William Carey Library.
  1970 *Church Growth and the Word of God.*
      Grand Rapids, Eerdmans.
  1972 *People Movements in Southern Polynesia.*
      Chicago, Moody Press.

TUGGY, A. L.
  1971 *The Philippine Church: Growth in a Changing Society.* Grand Rapids, Eerdmans.

TUGGY, A. L. and TOLIVER, Ralph
  1972 *Seeing the Church in the Philippines.*
      Manila, O.M.F. Publishers.

WAGNER, Peter
  1970 *The Protestant Movement in Bolivia.* South Pasadena, William Carey Library
  1972 *Frontiers in Missionary Strategy.*
      Chicago, Moody Press.
  1973 *Church/Mission Tensions Today.*
      Chicago, Moody Press.
  1974 *Stop the World I Want to Get On.*
      Glendale, Regal Press.
  1976 *Your Church Can Grow.* Glendale, Regal Press.

WINTER, Ralph
  1970 *The Twenty-five Unbelievable Years.*
      South Pasadena, William Carey Library
  1974 *Seeing the Task Graphically*

WOLD, Joseph C.
   1968   *God's Impatience in Liberia.* Grand Rapids, Eerdmans.

Appendix C
Distributing the Results of
A Church Growth Survey

A. *DEPOSIT A COPY OF THE SURVEY REPORT WITH:*

School of World Mission and Institute of Church Growth
Fuller Theological Seminary
135 N. Oakland Ave. Pasadena, Calif. 91101

The Missionary Research Library
3041 Broadway, New York, NY 10027

The Commission on World Mission and Evangelism
World Council of Churches
475 Riverside Dr. New York, NY 10027

The Secretary, Research Dept. CWME
Edinburgh House, 2 Eaton Gate
London S.W. England

The Evangelical Foreign Missions Assn.
1405 G. St. N.W. Washington, D.C. 20005

The Interdenominational Foreign Missions Assn.
54 Bergen Ave., Ridgefield Park, New Jersey

The Libraries of all schools and seminaries that would have interest in the study.

B. *SEND REVIEW COPIES TO:*

The International Review of Missions
150 route de Ferney
Geneva, Switzerland

Christianity Today
1019 Washington Bldg.
Washington, D.C. 20005

Church History
Swift Hall 306
University of Chicago
Chicago, Illinois 60637

Evangelical Missions Quarterly
Box 794
Wheaton, Illinois 60187

Missiology: An International Review
American Society of Missiology
135 N. Oakland Ave.
Pasadena, California 91101

Denominational publications of denominations involved in the study.

Ebbie C. Smith has served fifteen years as missionary to Indonesia. He served two terms as teacher in the Baptist Theological Seminary in Semarang, Indonesia, where he also directed the evangelistic extension program. Beginning in 1970, Smith worked in the area of Theological Education by Extension.

A native of Texas, Smith received the B.A. from Hardin-Simmons University in 1954 and the B.D. and Th.d. from Southwestern Baptist Theological Seminary in 1957 and 1961. In 1970 Smith was awarded the M.C. in Missiology from the School of World Mission and Institute of Church Growth, Fuller Theological Seminary. He is working toward a degree in Sociology at the University of Houston.

While on furlough, Smith is serving with the Missions Division of the Baptist General Convention of Texas, holding church growth seminars in Mexican Baptist Churches in Texas.

Books by the William Carey Library

General
The 25 Unbelievable Years 1945-1969 by Ralph D. Winter $2.95
The Birth of Missions in America by Charles L. Chaney $7.95p
Church Growth and Group Conversion by Donald A. McGavran $2.45p
Education of Missionaries' Children by D. Bruce Lockerbie $1.95p
Everything You Need to Know to Grow a Messianic Synagogue by Phillip E. Goble $2.45p
Growth and Life in the Local Church by H. Boone Porter $2.95p
Message and Mission: the Communication of the Christian Faith by Eugene Nida $3.95p
Reaching the Unreached: A Preliminary Strategy for World Evangelization by Edward Pentecost $5.95p
Verdict Theology in Missionary Theory by A. R. Tippett $4.95p

Area and Case Studies
Aspects of Pacific Ethnohistory by Alan R. Tippett $3.95p
The Baha'i Faith: Its History and Teachings by William Miller $8.95p
A Century of Growth: The Kachin Baptist Church of Burma by Herman Tegenfeldt $9.95c
Church Growth in Japan by Tetsunao Yamamori $4.95p
Circle of Harmony: A Case Study in Popular Japanese Buddhism with Implications for Christian Mission by Kenneth J. Dale $4.95p
A New Day in Madras by Amirtharaj Nelson $7.95p
People Movements in the Punjab by Margaret and Frederick Stock $8.95p
The Protestant Movement in Italy by Roger Hedlund $3.95p
Protestants in Modern Spain: the Struggle for Religious Pluralism by Dale G. Vought $3.45p
The Religious Dimension in Hispanic Los Angeles: A Protestant Case Study by Clifton Holland $9.95p
Solomon Islands Christianity: A Study in Growth and Obstruction by A. R. Tippett $5.95xp
Taiwan: Mainline Versus Independent Church Growth by Allen J. Swanson $3.95p
Understanding Latin Americans by Eugene Nida $3.95p

Theological Education by Extension
Designing a Theological Education by Extension Program by Leslie D. Hill $3.95xp
An Extension Seminary Primer by Ralph Covell and Peter Wagner $2.45p
Principles of Church Growth (programmed) by Weld and McGavran $4.95xp
Theological Education by Extension (revised edition) Ralph D. Winter $9.95p
The World Directory of Theological Education by Extension by Wayne C. Weld $5.95p 1976 Supplement only $1.95xp
Writing for Theological Education by Extension by Lois McKinney $1.45xp

Applied Anthropology
Becoming Bilingual: A Guide to Language Learning by Donald Larson and William A. Smalley $5.95xp
Bibliography for Cross-Cultural Workers by A. R. Tippett $4.95p, $5.95c
Christopaganism or Indigenous Christianity? by Tetsunao Yamamori and Charles Taber $5.95p
The Church and Cultures by Louis J. Luzbetak $5.95xp
Culture and Human Values: Writings of Jacob Loewen ed. by William A. Smalley $5.95p
Customs and Cultures: Anthropology for Christian Missions by Eugene A. Nida $3.95p
God's Word in Man's Language by Eugene Nida $2.95p
Manual of Articulatory Phonetics by William Smalley $4.95xp
Readings in Missionary Anthropology ed. by William Smalley $4.95xp